THE ETERNAL SAIL

CAMIL BUSQUETS I VILANOVA

THE ETERNAL SAIL

ALL PHOTOGRAPHS BY THE AUTHOR

For men of the sea

© EDIMAT BOOKS Ltd. London
is an affiliate of Edimat Libros S.A.
C/ Primavera, 35 Pol. Ind. El Malvar
Arganda del Rey - 28500 (Madrid) Spain
E-mail: edimat@edimat.es

Title: *The Eternal Sail*
Author: *Camil Busquets i Vilanova*

ISBN: 84-9794-045-8
Legal Deposit: M-48873-2004

PRINTED IN SPAIN

Contents

Following pages, Topsail schooner Pride of Baltimore.
Detail of the yards, crosstree and jib gaff.

Introduction

Nao Santa María I. General view of construction from the captain's cabin deck.

*F*or some time now, 'the return of the sail' has become fact - if not phenomenon. It is not a case of an increase in the number of sailing practitioners belonging to the generally known about common classes (ocean, cruising, dinghy, olympic, etc.), which are experiencing a 'boom' in spite of limitations and all sorts of problems that put obstacles in their paths. We are talking about a more classic, traditional cut of sail, more subtle and delicate. It is, in fact, the passion for sailing ancient ships once more. It is restoring and reforming more or less abandoned, true antiques into attractive, living crafts.

We are not only talking about the passion for sailing; it is in some way a dream, almost a longing, that while enjoying sailing, that pleasure is linked to ships that creak when they list, that have to be looked after and pampered, to which one must devote a much greater level of attention than that spent on fibreglass hulls; if anyone dares mention them in the same breath. These are ships whose rigging and sails consciously, valiantly spurn synthetic fibres, returning to cotton and

Nao Santa María. Construction of the forecastle and decking.

Nao Santa María I. General view of construction from the forecastle.

hemp. To sum it up, it is about going back to the heroic, glory days of sailing.

Evidently people whose whole lives revolve around this process cannot be considered 'normal'. Neither are they, nor do they wish to be. Their sensitivity does not allow such categorisation. The fact of the matter is, though, that with these ships, to know them is to love them. There can be no doubt as to the sailors' belief that all ships have a soul; the strangest, noblest souls belong to these ships, ancient but not old, veterans but not spent. Their owners and those that have had the immense honour of knowing and the indescribable pleasure of touching them will testify to it.

Furthermore, people's tendency to show anomalies in behaviour and character is undeniable. They often want something without realising that once upon a time they had it in the palm of their hand. Not only do they fail to realise that, but they make absolutely no concerted effort whatsoever to conserve what they had.

So it is with sailing ships. The Spanish sai-

Vessel Neptuno.
Main deck.

The lateen caravel Niña. General view of the starboard fashion piece (with sails).

In this respect as well, there is something worthy of praise, and that is the reconstruction of historical ships, disappeared long ago, which reveal to us some of the vaguer aspects of naval architecture, and despite creating more than one controversy, represent a valuable contribution to man's naval heritage. What a shame it is that, once part of that reconstruction has been completed, it has not been possible for them to be returned to the country where they were built.

Although comparisons are always detestable, we can but lament that Spain has proven to be so ungrateful to those ships that plied the seas under the Spanish flag, loaded with all kinds of cargoes. It is regrettable that these were often lost, along with the ship, and almost its memory. That is precisely where we find lacking the intense, unconditional love other countries feel for their maritime history.

ling fleet was one of the longest surviving that ever existed. Ships over one hundred years old were commonplace and during the sixties and seventies, not only did they number in their dozens, but were also made use of right until their last usable moment. The sad fact of it all does not lie there, though, but in the fact that there is almost no trace of those ships, mute testimonies of a historical period of splendour. They are now resting on Spanish coastal sea beds, cremated, blown up or simply ripped of their bottoms, if not buried under some new port jetty. Not all were unforgivably lost; luck would have it, to our shame, that some have survived in the hands of international philanthropists who had the sense to value what Spain rejected.

It should not be forgotten that this very maritime history is a very important part of a country's history, especially as far as Spain's is concerned, ruling all the seas of the world. Many a Spaniard crossed the seas in search of a more prosperous, pleasant life, first as colonisers and then, several centuries later, simple emigrants. Shouldn't at least gratefulness be reciprocated to the ships,

Xaloc. Attempt at the reconstruction of a felucca or ketch, from a sardine trawler.

Spanker cutter Scipio. Sailing hauling in to starboard, with spanker, small jib and flying jib raised.

and not the people, that made it possible?

At present, there is a group of sailors striving to recover a portion of all this lost maritime heritage. Sadly, in order to do so, the only ships they have at their disposal - although there are exceptions – are ones whose history is not as well-known or important as others already gone, or ones hailing from other countries apart from Spain. Moreover, there are those who, faced with

the great difficulties involved in owning and conserving an antique ship, plump for the easier solution of building or modifying a more modern one. They do this, though, with old technology and without using modern-day materials, which is in fact comprehensively prohibited.

To these true apostles to their passion, let us pay a most heartfelt tribute of admiration and envy.

PART I
Columbian ships

When Christopher Columbus discovered, or as some say bumped into, America, he did not only deliver to humanity a previously unknown world and another, great continent; the voyage also demanded drastic, radical change now that civilisation's nerve centres had been shifted. As a result, nations had to quickly learn to sail across oceans without being able to see land at all and thus shelter on a friendly, protective, or simply unhostile and risk-free coastline.

The Mediterranean, the Roman 'Mare Nostrum', was the very same sea in which so many and such different naval battles had been waged - from Salamina to Actium. It had been bloodied by innumerable skirmishes when not by 'world wars' - the Punic Wars, for example - and yet had already conceded some of its fame to the Atlantic coasts of Europe. Nevertheless, it was a major blow to lose overnight what it had held on to for so long (some consider the battle of Lepanto as the swan song) to the great Atlantic-crossing adventure.

This was not everything, of course; all naval and navigational technology in general had, in a few years, to make advances not made in centuries. Indeed, the ships available to marinas that were to participate in the discovery had no real ocean-going capacity. The world-renowned caravels and naos were not even 82 feet in length. Moreover, sailing across an enclosed sea like the Mediterranean, despite being risky, makes it very difficult to get lost as sooner or later you will come across some coast or other. The same does not apply to sailing an open, completely unknown ocean, which even with favourable winds took at least two months to cross.

Navigation up to the Middle Ages

The 'pax romana' imposed by Augustus after the battle of Actium ended more than one thousand years of war that had laid waste to the Mediterranean coastline. In spite of Roman civilisation's powerful land forces, they became respectable sailors and adept shipbuilders.

Nonetheless, as already mentioned, the closed nature of the Mediterranean and the dominating force in Europe being the land forces of the Roman legions, meant there was little call for great advances in naval technology. As such, sai-

Previous pages, the nao *Santa María I* sailing under full sail during ship trials. She flies mainsail, foresail, mizzen, topsail and spritsail.

ling in ancient times tended to be limited, preferring only the most favourable times of year. Ships were docked in secure ports during the winter to avoid hazards at sea. Boats did not measure 131 feet in length or 250 tonnes of displacement, although they were well suited to that kind of sea and navigation. They say that in the times of Constantine, though, an obelisk was transported from the Temple of the Sun, in Heliopolis, to Rome. The obelisk weighed 1,500 tonnes and was 115 feet long, and must therefore have required the building of a ship capable of taking such a load. Such a ship must have been the biggest in her time.

Despite their ability to build great ships, people tend to see the Romans as having brought very little of great importance to naval technology. For one thing, young Romans hungry for honour and glory tended to show more interest in land battle with the legions than maritime warfare; and for another, the scorn Romans tended to have for commerce, and merchants in general did not encourage them to devote time to sailing as a commercial venture. This meant that they only went to sea as a last resort and the crews on Roman vessels tended to be made up of foreigners (Phoenicians, Greeks, etc.) who, logically, were best acquainted with the art of navigation.

It is hardly surprising, then, that when Constantine the Great finished off Lucinius, in 323 AD, almost all the vessels – numbering more than 2,500 – taking part in the battle came from Rome's ally countries and cities, and were not actually Roman but Bithynian, Corinthian, Cypriote, Dorian, Egyptian, Phoenician, Greek, Jonian, etc.

Meanwhile, in northern Europe, the need to sail much more agitated, hostile waters than the Mediterranean – as a general rule, at least – led to ships that were quite different being built, using technology little resembling that of Spain.

In the Mediterranean, oar power in one or more rows (galleys and triremes) with or without sail – particularly in battles – was common as merchant propulsion or for war support ships - with one mast and square sails.

The lateen sail, despite its name, was not a sail that belonged to the Roman's repertoire. As regards hulls, Roman naval architecture immortalised boats with various rowing structures – there are still several theories about how the triremes

Building the frames. Frames construction with the corresponding design. Each frame is built from a double wooden frame, with the required shapes and qualities, taking care to make the most of the wood. *Right,* final design specifications and all forms and angles are checked. The frame is held apart by a piece of wood to stop it closing on itself.

Beginning of the framing. The frames are placed over the keel, supported by scaffolding of good supports and with the sternpost already in position. They are kept straight with struts, tools, and various assisting props.

Interior parts of the frame. General view of the framing with strakes and other parts in place.

worked - devoted uniquely to war, and just like the galley, with very little refinery (length: beam). In contrast, merchant trade was transported by the so-called *onerarioe ships*, which had a much wider beam (for which they were also known as *rontundae ships*).

The Greek and Roman Civilisations, contrary to the Phoenician, as inventors of the alphabet, devoted a great amount of written documentation to their ships. This was partly due to it being considerably important to understand the secrets of sailing to gain an appreciable military advantage.

The Romans built their ships with end to end sheeting, without exterior pins or juts. The strakes were joined to each other by a system known as *tenon and mortise*: first the interior billets (mortises) are attached and by inserting flat barbs of wood (tenons) and held in place by round wooden pins (belaying pins). They used a very particular system of construction known as first sheeting, which meant building from the outside in. First the outer surface of the sheeting was built to later incorporate the interior structural elements (keel, frames, etc.). It was normal to helm by steering oar and as such the rudder was not yet in use.

The Barbarians were another civilisation with their feet firmly on the ground even though they reached some parts by sea, and their invasion led to a considerable decline in naval architecture, plunging it into the dark ages.

Paradoxically, the arrival of the Vikings, the Arab invasion and then almost immediate reconquest initiated the gradual recovery of sailing on the Iberian Peninsula. In the rest of the Mediterranean, city-states greatly stimulated naval architecture. Large northern commercial cities like the Hanseatic League also gave rise to innovation

and advances, evidently for commercial reasons. Less typically, the crusades, with their considerable human traffic and transporting of knowledge of all kinds, also contributed to an exchange of naval technologies.

The Middle Ages undoubtedly led to a considerable amount of innovation and improvement to navigation and naval construction as a result of military expeditions of all kinds (Catalan-Aragonese expeditions to the East, etc.).

The Vikings brought their fast, light ship technology - shallow draft and raised sheeting - and their great, almost fearless expeditions to unknown lands, reaching Iceland, Greenland and even America. In the north itself, wooden hulk and cog ships were starting to appear. Sometime between the seventh and the ninth centuries the *first sheeting* system stopped being used and the traditional method of attaching the exterior sheeting to the keel and ribs system was introduced. The lateen sail became naturalised to the Mediterranean and at the end of the thirteenth century, the rudder was brought in (both features were probably Asian inventions brought to Europe by the Arabs). It was to replace the traditional double or single steering oars system.

During the middle of the fifteenth century there was a technological revolution in naval construction in the form of sheeting that enclosed the skeleton – something that, among other things, allowed larger copies of boats with the same characteristics to be built than before – and a variation in rigging that constituted a radical improvement: adopting several masts rather than just one. Not only did this allow ships to be propelled with greater displacement and faster speeds, but the greatest advantage the innovation afforded was better navigational control and the possibility of covering greater distances since manoeuvrability varied considerably. The single mast with one square sail made way for three trunks or masts –

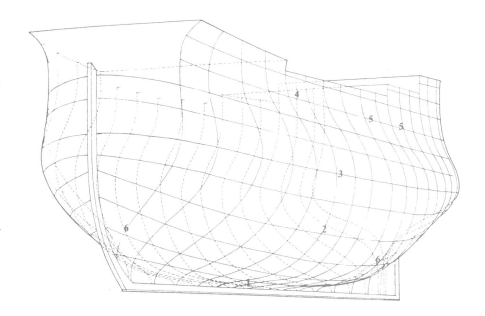

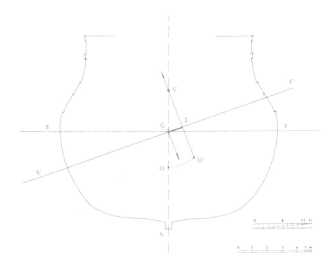

still in one piece at that stage – with three different sails. The foresail and the mainsail flew square; not so for the mizzen which did the same with a lateen sail. This resulted in greater capacity to beat into the wind – meaning heading into the wind on very tight courses. Ships could therefore then sail in winds that were not always favourable, something that boats at that time had not been able to do.

Another reason that notably contributed to the modification of the construction system and the increase in canvas was the need to load artillery onto ships. This happened, it would appear, around 1379, during the War of Chioggia between the Genoans and the Venetians. The arming of artillery on board small ships was very difficult, in equal parts due to the space available for such an enterprise and the inherent weakness of the vessels. To begin with, artillery could only be loaded at the bow of rowing ships (in the case of

galleys) forcing manoeuvering in order to position the cannons, and on top of that, with the recent addition of portholes it could start to be loaded at the sides, a system requiring good stability which small carriage boats could not provide.

Advances in humanity have always been strongly in keeping with commercial or military needs, the latter more so than the former, and as a result of the usual land routes with China being closed, commercial needs dictated that a route to the Far East via the south of Africa and the Indian Ocean had to be found. A change that made sea voyages considerably longer with the logical consequence of more crew and equipment.

One of the most enduring boats of the period was the cog – unique, as well, in that a votive offering model has enabled an almost complete understanding of the boat at the end of her long life. It was the kind of vessel whose evolution ran parallel to the period from the eleventh to the fifteenth century, and which, to a certain extent, encapsulated all the philosophy and naval architecture of the period.

Nothing other than a detailed account of this votive offering model will do it justice, because it is of truly great importance. It was exhibited for centuries in the San Simón hermitage at Mataró, near Barcelona, and is the oldest of boats conserved contemporary to the discovery of America; as a result its exceptional value is that of a unique document of the age, equally unrepeatable in naval archaeology, and which must have been built some time in the fifteenth century. It shed light on a series of points that had only been indicated in engravings and illustrations – not al-

View of the hull of a ship from the port bow. In this engraving we can see the general lines of the hull of a ship with 74 cannons. The continuous lines suggest the exterior line of the hull from her port side, the discontinuous lines from her starboard. **1.** Bottom or keel. **2.** Bilge. **3.** Maximum width (approximately corresponding to the draught line). **4.** Direction of the sheeting lines (corresponding approximately to the continuous horizontal lines). **5.** Area of the mizzenmast and mainmast support mounts. **6.** Entry and exit points for water.

Stability calculations. **XY.** List or vertical symmetry plain. **EF.** Draught of hull at rest. **E'F'.** Draught of listing hull. **C.** Meta-centre. **G.** Hull centre of gravity. **O.** Careening centre. **O'.** Careening centre corresponding to the E'F'. list. **GZ.** Transversal stability pair.
Graph scales; top: scale in feet; bottom: in metres.

evidence, together with advances in naval architecture, of some appreciable astronomical discoveries and a return to the heliocentric theories. These led to the conclusion that the Earth was a globe (which in conjunction with religious reform brought grave penalties to its propagators). It did not necessarily lead, though, to knowledge of lands beyond the Atlantic (Martin Beahaim's 1492 Earth globe).

Under such circumstances, Columbus' discoveries can only seem logical. Though having said that, his voyages should not be undervalued in the slightest.

The ships of the Discovery

The two most controversial, debated ships are, without a doubt, *Noah's Ark* and Christopher Columbus' *Santa María*.

We are not going to enter into discussion here about the practical or technological viability of *Noah's Ark*. To some extent, this boat's existence goes hand in hand with that of the Flood, both equally highly emotionally charged that they have little – if anything at all – to do with naval architecture.

Columbus' *Santa María* – and by extension the other two *Discovery* ships – are seriously, technologically controversial, and thus result in fierce, passionate discussions, theories and debates, although, on this occasion, there is one simple unarguable, undeniable fact: Columbus reached the New World. Just as there can be no doubt as to this, it is equally evident that he had to use a ship to do so. The forms and characteristics of that boat belong to the stuff of legend since in those days neither plans nor schemes were used in the construction of boats and no documentary evidence of any kind exists. Because of this, all we know about the boats is what we have learnt from certain historical accounts often lacking in form since they were written by people motivated by very different reasons. Something similar occurs with engravings and tapestries paid for by the nobleman of the moment, whose artistic inspiration does not always correspond with a total, absolute documentary or historical rigorousness.

Very illustrious names are linked to Columbus' ships and we dare not discuss the validity of their claims. They constructed many

ways calculable – like the moon shape of the bow, the construction of the stern and many interior details.

Little is known about that particular vessel and her sorrows. There can be no doubt though that she disappeared from her secular home during the first quarter of the last century, only to reappear at the Munich Antiques Market, in 1920, after having travelled to London and New York. Finally, she was bought by the Dutch millionaire Van Beuningen, who donated her to the renowned Prins Hendrik Museum in Rotterdam.

To look at, the cog was a short, rounded vessel, lighter than the nao and with greater manoeuvrability, and was thus preferred, equipped with a forecastle, quarterdeck and main deck lower than the nao, though high enough above her draught line.

Carrying capacity varied greatly, in some cases as great as 1,500 tonnes (70,000 gallons) and crews up to 120 men (140 in battle). The precise dates of the first and the last cogs are not known, although we do know that there were still some during the middle of the sixteenth century, even if in 1604, no important references to work on cogs can be found. One cog truly worthy of acclaim was the *San Clemente*, launched in 1331 in Barcelona, which it is said, had three decks and a crew of more than 500 men.

Arabic culture and civilisation brought great astronomical and mathematical knowledge to navigation, allowing greater awareness of the boat's position. This was also necessary given how much harder sea voyaging had become. In the fifteenth century, at least in the second half, there is

Transporting to the outdoor slipway brought with it a truly logistical operation. The streets had to be cleared of cars, lifted out when they blocked the way.

19

(about a dozen) boats of different types and appearances (*Santa Marías, Pintas* and *Niñas*), to prove the various theories that each historian proposes, but where there do not appear to be too many differences with respect to the two smaller boats, the *Pinta* and the *Niña,* the same cannot be said of the *Santa María.* This is probably due to the fact that she never returned, allowing interminable discussions and heated commentaries in favour of this or that theory, which still do not appear to have been definitively resolved.

The most universally accepted reconstructions have been those of the fourth Centenary (Cesáreo Fernández Duro), who thought the Santa María to be a nao, although her stern was flat; that of Julio Guillén Tato (former Director of the Madrid Naval Museum) as a caravel, without forecastle, and with a very high bowsprit; that of Jose María Martínez-Hidalgo y Terán (Director of the Royal Shipyards of Barcelona), also a nao; and last of all, that of the fifth Centenary State Commission, which also looks like a nao. This last commission also ordered the repeated reconstruction efforts of the other two Columbian ships, whose significance we shall see later.

Indeed, Barcelona's *Santa María* was unsuspectedly succeeded by another replica – completely matching in all other details – commissioned by a Japanese company, based on the argument that at the end of the day, Columbus was trying to get to Cathay and the Far East.

The three main types of Spanish ship that existed at the end of the fifteenth century were the carrack, the nao and the caravel. The carrack was the largest, even though some people do not differentiate it from the nao. Yet Fernández Duro states Isabel the Catholic's provision dated on the 15th October, 1502, which establishes a certain difference between the carrack and the rounded nao. The Portuguese may have been her creators, with her name deriving from *navis carricata* – loaded ship – that is a ship specially designed to carry a large cargo. The usual rigging on the carrack seems to have the three masts (fore, main and mizzen) rigged with square sails on the first two and a lateen on the last. The main mast also flew a well-sized topsail, and in spite of having a bowsprit, it would appear that no sail was rigged on to this pole. Her hull, with a rounded stern but not quite attaining the classic galley stern, decked two powerful castles, a particularly protruding forecastle and a more contained quarterdeck. As regards her displacement, this seems to have varied greatly, from 100 to 400 tonnes, with certain notable ex-

ceptions, the *Chronique de Louis XII* mentions a carrack, the *Charente*, armed with 300 artillery pieces and 1,200 soldiers to which the needs for service on board had to be added. At the end of the sixteenth century, the Portuguese had great cargo carracks with up to 2,000 tonne carrying capacity, carrying out increased commerce with their Asian goods. It would appear that there was also a lateen carrack whose sails were made up of this type of sail.

The nao appeared in the twelfth century, as a boat with just one mast and often platform sheeting. Later, in the fifteenth century, ships were characteristically built weighing around 600 tons, armed with two masts with square rigging (foresail and main) and a third (mizzen) with a lateen sail. Many naos were also fitted with a topsail in the main hoisted up from an ample top. The projecting and lofty forecastle, originally the positioning point of archers, crowned a hull that used stretched out or full sheeting. The stern, originally flat, became increasingly curved until it was completely round. Due to the longevity of the nao it

The Santa María I, still on the transport trailer, in the future outdoor slipway where she will be completed before being launched.

The Santa María I touches water for the first time in her life. It is the most solemn, important moment in any boat's history.

21

is not surprising that it continued evolving, shifting from oar steering (one in the Atlantic and two in the Mediterranean) to rudder. One historical note on the Atlantic nao's sails is the fact that it started to use reef bands in its sails, while those in the Mediterranean changed the sails themselves altogether. The Mediterranean nao used to carry lateen rigging, and in this way they transported the numerous armies of San Luis to the Holy Land. Generally they had two decks that ran the whole length of the ship; the smaller one, the

hold, was where the heaviest loads, such as provisions and munition, were placed. The space between the two decks was used for transporting the horses, and a third which ran from one side to the other only covered the castles.

This variety seems to have derived from the Moorish caravels. It was a kind of ship that, because of the shape of its hull and its type of rigging, was particularly suited to beating windward, that is, sailing with the wind to a greater or lesser degree at the bow and tacking frequently.

The principle and most noticeable characteristic of its hull was the absence of a castle, taking the deck right up to the stem. There were round (or square sails) and lateen caravels, the latter bearing two or three masts. The fact that they sailed close haul (with the wind at the bow) better than the naos and carracks - Columbus speaks of close haul sailings of 67.5 degrees (6 fourths), with certain stories of the time telling how a caravel tacked at full speed *with the same security as if it was being sailed with oars* - made them particularly suitable for the long days of exploration. Yet their load capacity, limited through necessity, made habitability and carrying equipment and provisions difficult. Its hull was narrower, having a greater refining ratio than that of the naos and carracks of the same length. There are authors who consider that the name 'caravel' only refers to its discovery capacity. It seems that the caravel rarely exceeded 100 - 200 tons and although its golden age coincided with the end of the fifteenth century and first third of the sixteenth century, by the end of the latter it was in decline and disappeared completely in the seventeenth century.

Evidently, the most important ships at the end of the fifteenth century did not fail to record certain similar characteristics that occasionally lead to error and confusion. If on top of that one adds the lack of reliable documentation perhaps it is easy to see the reason for frequent argument and controversy regarding the subject.

This scarce diffusion of the different characteristics would seem to be related to the wide range of laws that existed regarding the matter impeding the communication of their secrets under severe penalty. The penalties that were written down in the Justinian code remained in force for several centuries afterwards. A bylaw of the king of Aragon dated 11th June, 1424 in Barcelona prohibits: "*...in particular, the Trade and Guild of Valencian carpenters from showing their art to a Moslem, a Jew or an unbeliever, be he captive or free, the objective of this being that when he returns to his own country he will not be able to build rowing or other kinds of craft.*" But some historians tell of the secretism and confidentiality was not limited just to the architectural knowledge of the ships, but also extended to that of navigation and courses. Regarding this, Fernández Duro says that the king of Portugal, "*...having been displeased by a pilot and two sailors, fled towards Castilla,*

pursuing the men and having all of them killed except the pilot whose mouth he had sewn up so that he could not talk until he arrived in Ebora, where he was chopped up into pieces."

It is clear that considering such punishment, there must have been strong resistance to communicating any type of secret because if one king acted in this manner, it is unlikely that others would have done differently. With just the representation of the ships' forms in drawings or plans, something which started to become widespread from the sixteenth century onwards, a certain diffusion could not be avoided.

Whatever the case, in later times, including our own, an effort has been made to maintain confidentiality concerning certain characteristics that affect the performance of a ship, whether for reasons of trade, sport or simply because of the name or sponsor. And just as there are boats of the type that don't exist or of which plans were made - such as a few practice boats that are still in service in the port of Barcelona, built by Cardona Shipyard in recent years - there are also regatta boats, such as those used in the America's Cup, whose dynamic forms are jealously guarded as if they were military secrets. Likewise, the propellers of the top competition Off-Shore catamarans are jealously protected under canvases as soon as they appear out of the water.

Whatever happened, it would seem beyond all doubt that Columbus had three ships and that they were greater than had originally been imagined - which doesn't mean that once seen they wouldn't appear scandalously small - and that all of them ended up with square rigging. As for their appearance, the *Santa María* was a nao, that is, with a projecting castle at the bow and contained within the stern superstructure, a round stern with the rudder in the central gangway and a rigging consisting of three one-piece masts, foremast with foresail; main - with top - with main and topsail; mizzen with lateen and bowsprit with spritsail, to which two bonnets were added on certain occasions.

As far as its measurements and construction characteristics are concerned, José María Martínez-Hidalgo y Terán, a great scholar and undoubtedly one of the greatest authorities on the matter, describes those of the *Santa María* as: length of deck, 77.42 feet; maximum beam, 25.98; stanchion, 12.63; draft, 6.88.

The Santa María I Mainly finished in wood, ready for its formal launch. This took place on 14th July, 1989, coincidentally the second centenary of Bastille Day and national French holiday.

In the building of a vessel as large as the *Santa María*, a great quantity of trees of all types (holm oak, oak, ash, pine, beech, etc.) was used, with total weights of up to 500 - 600 tons, the greater part of which was wasted or ended up as fuel for the heaters or fires in which the wood was curved. One can only understand the savage deforestation that took place in the Iberian and European forests in general when one considers that construction had to keep up with demand from the American continent for whole fleets of ships that also had to be defended against the attacks of any that tried to capture or sink them. The lack of wood became so urgent that, later on, in more knowledgeable centuries, wood was either brought over from American forests to Spanish shipyards or the ships themselves were built in the same place, as logically this was more practical.

The hull was covered in end to end sheeting, although the sheeting of the castle sides was made up of platform. Its sides were protected by strong, thick bands that stretched from the sternpost up to the stem itself, with thick webbing extending

from one of the straps to the edge of the gunwale. The thickness of the sheeting was about 3 in with caulked seams made of burlap and tar. The frames were double and joined to the keel with floors. The beams, which were sturdy and quite curved, were steadied to the frames by sleepers and counter sleepers. Nevertheless, such a robust construction could still become dislocated and would not withstand lengthy voyages on rough seas, which is why it was advantageous to keep it well looked after and in good shape. This explains why ship carpenters and a good assortment of tools and wood supplies were always carried on board. Besides, it didn't take much to cause serious damage, since a leak due to loss of water tightness in the hull would become a serious problem, as it would have to be repaired with the resources on board and during the voyage. Once the vessel reached one of America's scarce islands, the problem became less serious as there was a better chance of careening or repairing the ship in some sheltered bay that looked sufficiently hospitable.

Naval and scientific consequences of the discovery

The discovery of rich lands beyond the ocean represented a series of nautical advances, happening almost against the will of the sailors themselves.

The voyages became increasingly longer, which created a need for larger crews and, consequently, far greater quantities of provisions and equipment of every kind, as ships had to be more self-sufficient than in the past. If the outgoing voyage meant travelling with a heavy load, besides carrying numerous products manufactured in the mother country and others not existing in the New World, the return voyage would be undertaken with such an overload of riches that it was almost impossible to travel. This resulted in ships with greater displacement capacity and speed being used, with the aim of increasing the profitability of the voyage whilst at the same time making it shorter. A further aspect that could also be an advantage of a shorter journey was a better or greater manoeuvrability. As navigation between Europe and America was carried out mainly according to the winds of constant direction, anything that allowed for greater manoeuvrability of the ships was welcome, as it would make shorter courses or different routes possible. And if that was beneficial on voyages between the European and American continents, for those of circumnavigation and exploration of the Pacific that followed immediately after, it became absolutely essential.

This meant that ships in the century that followed the discovery of America increased in size or displacement in great proportion and it was not strange to see ships of more than 1,000 tons from the mid-sixteenth century onwards, quadrupling perfectly the displacement of Columbus's own flagship. But building such large vessels required a much greater quantity of sails at one's disposal, which led to the use of compound masts (the first ship to bear one such mast was *Henri Grace a Dieu*, England, 1536) or masts consisting of two pieces (lower and topmast) which were replaced a short time later by the definitive three piece mast (lower, topmast and topgallant mast), which carried a vast quantity of sails as it was neither feasible nor practical to make and use enormous ones.

At the same time, hull construction systems

General view of the Santa María I, the painting almost finished, by its stern line handler, viewed from its port.

became much stronger. By increasing the sail's traction effort, an increase in the hull's structural resistance became vital. If the hulls were not built in this way they would eventually get knocked out of position, causing a great number of leaks that could lead to the ship sinking. However, sailing with larger hulls that could stand up to the crests of the successive waves also required something similar, in the same way as sailing on ocean waters, with waves of considerable height, required an enlarged freeboard, and this had a bearing on total increases of weight and displacements.

Oceanic voyages in the sixteenth and seventeenth centuries forced improvements in many details of life on board, as well as in shipbuilding and the art of sailing.

Although the food a sailor could find himself eating at the end of a long and difficult voyage would not even be considered fit for pigs these days, out of necessity, the food on board had to be varied. This was often in spite of the commander's desires. But the arrival on board of scurvy or dysentery would lead to serious or fatal consequences, including for the commanders themselves. All in all, life on board continued to be a hard test until at least the end of the eighteenth century or the beginning of the nineteenth century.

One of the aspects that changed most in ocean voyages was undoubtedly the art of sailing itself. If sailing by means of good knowledge of the stars was already well known in the times of the Greeks, Romans and Arabs, and made use of at any opportunity, this later became mandatory on setting off on any important voyage in which an error, however small it may have seemed, could lead to locating, or not, the port of destination; or maybe not even finding land and ending up lost on an immense ocean. Consequently navigation instruments were improved to perfection as was astro-

Making of a mast (jib). Extraction of the surplus wood, at a later stage to the marking of the squadron and draught of surplus to make the work of the adze easier.

nomical, mathematical, and cartographic knowledge, the use of which provided greater security. Discovering the New World and the oceans surrounding it had a similar importance for knowledge of that time as that of modern astronomical knowledge has had in our own. At least on scientific or technological levels, as with other more tangible ones, the population and society of the Modern Age reaped many more direct benefits which were reflected in their own every day lives.

Reconstructions of Columbus ships

At least a dozen Columbus ships have been reconstructed, quite closely at least. With many of them, this was due to historical documental reasons, but others for certain less scientific purposes. The history and facts of the best known, or most important, are the following:

Naos of the IV Centenary (1892)

Destined for the fourth Centenary commemorations of Christopher Columbus' voyages, a replica with a displacement of 233 tons was built in the naval dockyard at La Carraca. A board was formed, presided by the inspector general of engineers of the Armada, D. Casimiro Bona, who also carried out the project of the ship in which D. Cesáreo Fernández Duro, captain of the ship, D. Rafael Monleón and Sirs Fernández Guerra and De la Rada Delgado, both History academics, Puente, the engineer who drew the plans, and Cardona - the ship carpenter who also built replicas of the *Pinta* and the *Niña* all took part.

On 22nd February 1893, at D. Victor Concas, the captain of the frigate's, command, it started its voyage in Santa Cruz, Tenerife, arriving at San Juan in Puerto Rico on 30th March. Within sight of the island of Cuba, the cruiser *Jorge Juan* took up the towing line and towed it to Havana, where it would continue its voyage to New York towed by the *Reina Regente,* and here it underwent a naval review on 1st May. Towed by the *Newark,* a North American cruiser, it sailed around San Lorenzo, arriving in Chicago to participate in the World Columbus Exhibition, anchoring alongside the *Pinta* and the *Niña,* in Jason Park.

If at first it was thought that the ships would return to Havana, where they were supposed to

Masting. The main mast and the topsail on the ground ready to be fitted. In the background, two parts of the main yard being put together.

remain as a form of record, finally, on 12th September, 1893, they were handed over by Spain to the United States. All of them met with a tragic end. The *Niña* sunk in 1918 due to a leak, was refloated, and then scrapped. In 1919 a fire destroyed the *Pinta*. The same fate also put paid to the *Santa María* in 1953 and the damage was such that it was decided it should be scrapped.

The caravel of TN. Guillén (1929)

This was the only caravel project of the whole series of reconstructions. It was built by Echevarrieta Shipyard and Larrinaga of Cadiz, according to D. Julio Guillén Tato's plans. Tato was the ship lieutenant of the Spanish Armada and later director of the Naval Museum, Madrid. It became highly controversial because of its caravel project, when numerous experts on the matter expressed themselves in favour of a nao, an opinion which he agreed with for a long time before seemingly reconsidering.

The main reason for the reconstruction was to contribute to building up and enhancing the splendour of the 1929 Ibero-American Exhibition, in Seville, where it remained until the closure. It then went on to join the ranks of the Armada, under the command of TN. Guillén himself.

The initial idea belonged to D. Torcuato Luca de Tena. In later conversations it was shown to General D. Miguel Primo de Rivera, who transmitted it to the Naval Minister, Admiral Cornejo. Building took five months, finally being towed from Cadiz to Seville by the gunboat *Laya,* where their majesties The King and Queen awaited it on board the cruiser *Reina Victoria Eugenia.*

Being towed once again by the *Laya,* in June 1939, it was transported to Huelva where it became the Columbus Museum, being transferred by the Armada to the National Board of Tourism in December of the same year. A travel project along the coasts of several American countries was rejected, remaining by and large ignored until 1939, when it returned to the ranks of the Armada which, in 1943, decided to tow it to the Atlántida Shipyard in Valencia, with the intention of caulking it. The operation was abandoned due to its high cost (one million pesetas at the time), causing a loss in the List of Navy Ships at the end of 1943. While being towed by the transporter *Tarifa* it sunk on route from Valencia to

Rigging and standing rigging. Start of the assembly of the shrouds.

Nao Santa María I. Sailing tests; preparation and manoeuvre of letting out the main.

Two images of the *Santa María Nao* sailing during his sea tests (Bercelona, 24 of July 1990), with the main mainsails, the foremast, the mizzen mast, the topsail and the spritsail hoisted.

Caravel Niña A. Finished, moored in one of the quays at Cartagena's naval dockyard. Note how the rigging is already finished but it is still without sails.

Caravel Niña A. Detail of the starboard shrouds or standing rigging of the jib. Notice the absence of deadeyes and lanyards in the classical style.

Cartagena, on the same latitude as Villajoyosa, due to the prevailing bad weather and the bad state its careening was in.

II Caravel of TN. Guillén (1951) for "Alba de América"

In 1951 the Valencian shipbuilders Lacomba built a second *Santa María* according to Guillén's plans, and which was built solely due to the shooting of the film "Alba de América" ("Dawn of America").

This is said to have been led by D. Enrique Tortosa, at that time director of the Empresa Nacional Elcano shipyard in Manises, near Valencia.

When filming was finished the ship was towed

to Barcelona by the hydrograph *Juan de la Cosa* and anchored in Muelle de Atarazanas (Atarazanas Wharf), near the statue of Columbus and next to the junk *Rubia*, which for many years was a veritable tourist attraction. In 1957, the Ministry of the Navy passed it on to Barcelona Provincial Council, who placed it in the authority of the Museu Marítimo de las Reales Atarazanas (Royal Shipyard Maritime Museum), having been used in another two films.

Given that at that time the director of the museum was D. José María Martínez-Hidalgo, a fanatical defender of the idea of it being a nao, the caravel was soon modified to the form of a nao, with the forecastle projecting at the bow. It maintained this appearance for many years.

According to what was said on many occasions, and owing to the short life expectancy it had been given at the beginning (a film shoot), this Santa María was built with materials that were not made to last (pine, etc). Although beautifully made, its maintenance cost a large amount of the museum's annual budget, though it did undoubtedly become one of the best known pieces and most visited by tourists.

It turned into a target of various political demands of nationalistic assemblies, being the object of several attacks, in particular around 12th October, Columbus Day. Finally, the attack carried out at the end of 1989 was more successful than previous attempts and a serious fire broke out affecting the main deck, quarterdeck and admiral's chamber. Considering the high repair costs and predictable repetition of attacks, and perhaps also due to the fact that the museum's new management was looking to put it to other uses, it was decided that the caravel would be sunk. Towed out

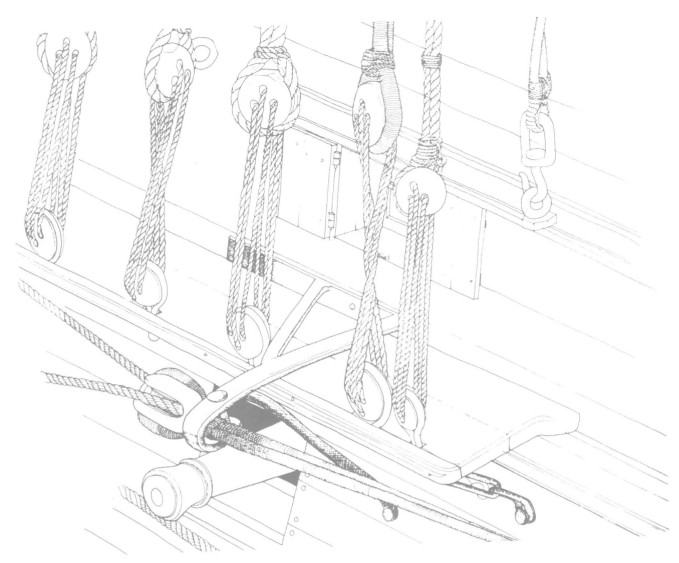

Close up of chain wales of mizzen mast on a 74 cannon ship. The lower deadeyes are secured to the hull by chainplates; the upper ones are rigged to the shrouds (the one furthest to the right to a backstay) and it is kept tight all over the rigging board by means of the lanyards (two of which appear with half a turn and a whole turn). The hook, secured to the gunwale, further to the right corresponds to the halyard of the mizzen royal, and the single block nearer the front – attached to a U-shaped framework with the open side closed by a rivet – to some mast rigging or specific strap.

as far as the artificial biotope at Maresme by a tug boat from the port of Barcelona, it was sunk in front of Calella lighthouse at the end of the summer of 1990. It appeared to be reluctant to meet its fate and had to be helped using a large quantity of rocks from a nearby breakwater.

The naos of Martínez-Hidalgo/Cardona (1963 and 1968)

The previously mentioned director of Barcelona Maritime Museum, D. José María Martínez-Hidalgo y Terán, studied the subject of the *Santa María* caravel for over ten years, carrying out several trials, tests and corrections with scale models. The reward of these studies was the commission,

in 1963, of a reconstruction of the *Santa María* destined for the New York World Fair of 1964-1965, through the prestigious Smithsonian Institution.

Construction was executed outside and finished within a few months, carried out by Cardona Shipyard, the company that had already built the two replicas of the *Pinta* and the *Niña* for the IV Centenary. It was boarded on the German merchant ship *Neudenfels* which took it to New York, where it was transported on to Meadow Lake on a platform.

Although it was said that its final destiny would be its return to Spain sailed by a Spanish crew, at the end of the fair it was instead transferred to Washington where, for some time, it was left floating on the River Potomac. In 1969 it was

Caravel Niña B. Modern type rudder wheel as well as modern controls and magnetic compass on the deck. The manoeuvring difficulties that the traditional system involved called for a modification. The whole control set could be dismantled, often the case when entering a port.

Caravel Pinta in Barcelona, during the 29th Salón Náutico International in1990, moored in the Muelle de España in the port of Barcelona.

transported to Saint Louis, where it presumably remains to this day.

The other *Santa María* was also constructed by Cardona Shipyard, under the supervision of Martínez-Hidalgo himself, during 1968, and commissioned by the Corporación de Fomento de la República de Venezuela (Republic of Venezuela Development Corporation).

After arriving at Port Cabello it went on to La Guayra where it was fitted out as the Museo del Descubrimiento (Discovery Museum), along with several dioramas and other atmospheric details. Currently it can be found in Caracas Central Park.

The ships of the V Centenary (1987-1992)

For the fifth Centenary of the Discovery a new State Commission was formed, endowed with numerous resources controlled by the General State Budget, which organised various commemorative acts.

One result of their activities was the construction of a new series of replicas of the Columbus ships. These were two complete fleets which, in order to make their identification easier, we shall call A and B and whose shipyard constructors were: *Santa María* A: Viudes Shipyard plc, of Barcelona; *Santa María* B: Reunidos Shipyard, plc, of Isla Cristina (Huelva). *Pinta* A: Reunidos Shipyard, plc, of Isla Cristina (Huelva); *Pinta* B: Shipyard Joaquín Castro, Ltd. Co., of La Guardia (Pontevedra). *Niña* A and B: Workshop of Ramo de Casco of the Military Arsenal, in Cartagena (Murcia). The historical project of the ships is that of the specialist historian, the previously mentioned, D. José María Martínez-Hidalgo y Terán. The construction project, as well as the total supervision of the work, was carried out by CN. José Luis López Martínez, naval engineer of the Spanish Navy.

Building two identical groups tied in with the request that one group should remain in Spain and the other in America. But in the end, the

ships in both places did not form homogenous groups as they became mixed up.

The first group (with the *Niña* B), after a long voyage around the Spanish coast, visited the 29th Barcelona International Nautical Exhibition, after which it went on to Marseille and then Italy. On route it was accompanied by the *Cartagena* a tug boat belonging to the navy. On finishing its voyage, it remained on show in the Universal Exhibition in Seville and can presently be seen in Palos de la Frontera, in the Cadiz region.

The second group (with the *Niña* A), carried out an Atlantic crossing emulating Columbus's earlier feat. The group was escorted by the navy patrol boats *Serviola* and *Centinela.* After the crossing they visited several countries and ports, finally arriving in New York on 14th July, 1992, coinciding with the great regatta Columbus-92. Currently the group is moored in Corpus Christi, Texas, with the Texan state in charge of maintenance, although it continues to be Spanish property.

There was a third *Santa María,* known as the

Japanese. Japan, the exotic country which Columbus had tried to reach, considered that it should form part of the acts in the V Centenary. For this reason it was decided to build another replica of the *Santa María,* which this time, would reach Columbus's Cathay or Cipango. It set sail for Barcelona at the beginning of November, 1990, on a voyage that would last eight months (along the route of the Panama Canal), escorted by a ship belonging to the Japanese Maritime Administration and finally arriving in Kobe.

The designer and sponsor of the work was the Japanese industrialist millionaire, Haruki Kadokawa, an able and active captain of a group of more than a dozen Japonese companies.

Other Replicas

Besides the various official replicas, or those whose existence and construction became on the whole well known, the following also seem to be of interest:

La Marigalante. In the mid-eighties, the

Spanish navigator and merchant captain Vital Alsar ordered a slightly unusual replica to be built. *La Marigalante*, after the captain of Columbus's second voyage, with which he sailed from South America (where it was built) to Spain. As the ship incorporated considerable variations (it used flying jibs instead of spritsails, spanker sails in the mizzen instead of lateen, etc.) in its rigging, along with a certain amount of decorative licence (figurehead at the bow, etc.) that was never used in the period, it is not often included in the group of Columbus replicas.

Its present whereabouts are unknown, and the possibility of it having been scrapped has not been ruled out.

Niña lateen with three masts. In the same decade, though perhaps slightly earlier, Cadiz Provincial Council constructed a caravel with three masts and entirely lateen rigging. The project was carried out in Barbate de Franco (Cadiz) under the direction of a lecturer at the Cadiz nautical school who was also captain of the merchant navy. It was a ship whose aim was to demonstrate certain specific theories, with more maritime than historical criteria, seeming to possess great sailing qualities although its various voyages were of no great importance. What is clear is that it was ex-cellent at sailing close haul (which ties in with the characteristics normally attributed to the caravel) and it was said to reach and surpass 15 knots, a fair speed considering it was sail only and carried no auxiliary motor.

After a few years of constant mooring in Puerto Sherry, it was moved to the port of Rota and moored there. Its long exposure to the elements (in 1993 it was still in Rota, totally exposed to the Andalusian sun and the high temperature of the water) and detailed but infrequent maintenance, seem to make a long life expectancy very unlikely.

Bartolomeu Dias. The Portuguese also wanted to take part in the saga of Columbus ships - after all, the Portuguese were also discoverers and colonizers in the sixteenth century as well as opening up the route to the East - so they built their own replica.

Not much is known about the *Bartolomeu Dias,* a lateen caravel with two masts. In 1992, it made a voyage around the Mediterranean. It appears that it was also built in order to show the great sailing qualities of the caravel. For this reason, a replica was designed according to the most classical documentation that existed and apparently it became the archetype of the Portuguese caravel used by its navigators.

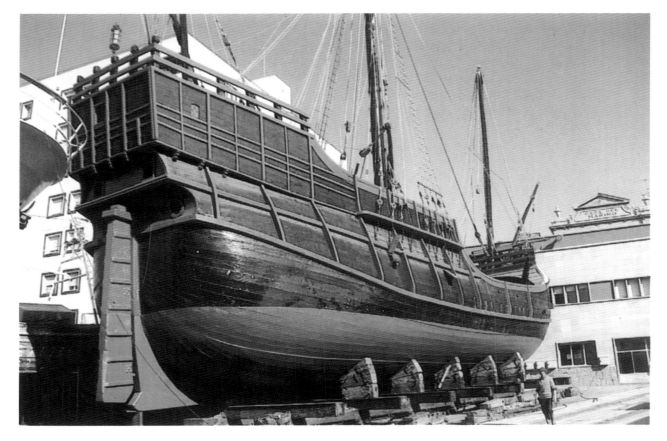

Nao Santa María (the caravel from the film "Alba de América", later converted into a nao) careening in the dry dock in the port of Barcelona, a little more than a year before its receiving its last attack.

Nao Santa María (the caravel from "Alba de América", later converted into a nao), totally bereft of mast, half scrapped and with no main deck, silhouetted against Montjuic, a few days before it was permanently sunk in front of Calella lighthouse.

Perspective view of the stern of a 74 cannon ship. In this drawing, in which only certain parts have been partially drawn or left out (such as the frames), one can appreciate the fineness and purity of the hull's water outlet lines as much as the complex construction of the hull itself.

P38-39: Detail of the main mast of the ship *Victory*.

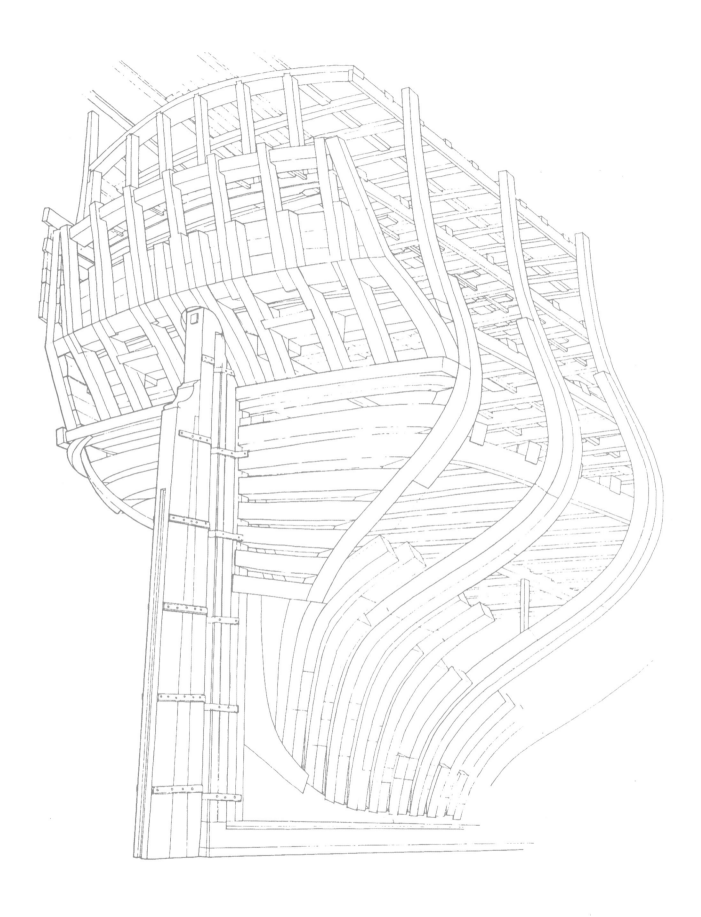

PART II
Vestiges of the Past

Navío Victory, on show within a dry dyke at the British naval base at Portsmouth. The Royal Navy keeps it in fully working order and in a perfect state of repair, now at the proud age of two centuries old.

Navío Victory, seen from starboard fashion piece. Constant maintenance can be clearly seen in the main mast (topmast and topgallant masts and all their yards missing), taken down for maintenance.

There are many ships that throughout history have sailed the seven seas. And among them there are also many that, for one reason or another, are particularly interesting, with some cases being truly notorious.

Naval archaeology has enabled man, since a time in the distant past, to discover much about the ships of a specific culture. But this has always been from on land sites, as diving technology was not sufficiently advanced. Even so, ships of great value and very interesting pieces have been found that have led to understanding a great number of details.

But it was not until after the Second World War that naval archaeologists, helped by the most modern research technology and submarine recovery, managed to recover and leave in excellent

Detail of the deck and jib mast of the Warrior. Its careful and perfect construction can clearly be seen.

condition, ships that had disappeared in well-known circumstances and whose position was, to a certain point, common knowledge. However, this does not mean to say that these rescue missions were easy. It was necessary to use very sophisticated processes in order to recover as much as was possible of the boat in question.

On land discoveries

The most habitual sources of naval archaeology used to be, in general, somewhat heterogeneous and included anything from receptacles and written or oral descriptions to bas-reliefs and mosaics, so there was little likelihood of coming across a ship - or the little that might have remained of one - buried in a favourable area.

Tombs and votive offerings (models made in compliance with a promise) constituted another source, the former being somewhat necrophilic and the latter totally spiritual, which also helped to reveal the appearance of ships that sailed the seas of earlier times, although always under the common denominator of the model of a ship. The best-known are: the boat of silver from Ur (4000 years BC); the ships in the tomb of Tutankhamen (1360 BC) and the Coca de Mataró or Nao Catalana, which was referred to in an earlier section.

Regarding what is referred to as to real ships, found in varying states of preservation, and on land excavations, or drainage operations, the following should be mentioned: the boat of Nydam (1853); the Viking ships of Tuna (1867), Gokstad (1880) and Oseberg (1903); the Nemi galley (1931) and on an indigenous and lesser well-known level, the so-called boat of Gavá (1990), a town near Barcelona, the silence surrounding which lead us to believe that further comment is called for.

The boat of Gavá

During excavations carried out for the construction known as the Olympic Rowing Canal, destined for the 1992 Olympic Games in Barcelona, set in the municipal mines of Gavá and Castelldefels in the delta of the Llobregat, in a site known as Les Sorres (The Sands) – where there appears to have been an anchorage between the fourth century BC and the fifth century AD, and

View from the bow and starboard of the battleship Warrior *as a floating exhibition in Portsmouth.*

from which many traces and pieces of considerable importance - a boat measuring about twenty-six feet in length, by two in breadth was discovered, which was dated back to some time around the fourteenth or fifteenth century. The finding, which appeared to be in an excellent state of preservation until it was partially destroyed by the action of the machines, consists of a small cabin, very near the bow, constructed directly over the frame. As there was not much time to finish the work, the ship was systematically excavated, dismantled, numbered and packaged. The wooden fragments were moved to the Servicio de Arqueología de la Generalitat de Catalunya (The Catalan Government Archaeology Service) in Pedret, near Girona, and nothing else was heard about the case.

Very little is said or known about the discovery, as the circumstances of where and how it was found did not permit a thorough, detailed inspection of the surroundings. Time was running out as the work on the canal had been slowed down but not interrupted. It is therefore quite likely that the importance of the discovery wasn't fully exploited - in the end an order of priority had to be established - which was very unfortunate as a boat from the Early Middle Ages, in the perfect condition it was said to be, seems an important, if not unique, archaeological opportunity. In any case, the fact is that this can sadly be considered as an example or reference point of how different the interest Spain shows towards the sea and ships is compared with certain other countries, as we will shortly discover. At least on particular levels of bodies or institutions.

The Maritime Discoveries

Reaching a sunken boat entails considerable difficulties. Apart from the fact that water is a hostile element for man, there is also the added problem of the complicated equipment required to extract the mud and sand, and the precarious state of decomposition of the wood through prolonged

Detail of the pin rack of the foresail mast of the *Warrior.*

contact with sea water. Therefore the work has to be done very carefully so that the hull, or what remains of it, does not break up on being handled or exposed to the atmosphere.

It wasn't until recently that expensive, modern technology in exploration and submarine recovery has been used decisively in naval archaeology. The following extractions are the most notable:

Wasa. A Swedish warship with 64 cannons, admiral ship of the fleet, sunk near Beckholmen, beside Stockholm, on 10th August, 1628, when carrying out its first and last voyage. It was the pride of the Wasa dynasty and of its king, Gustavus II Adolphus, who suffered greatly from this blow.

Faulty righting, due to too much high weight, made the ship heel over excessively, bringing water on board through the gun ports of the lower artillery. It sunk before the eyes of an astonished crowd, who had come to see the sight of such a majestic ship set sail on its maiden voyage. Indeed, it certainly was a spectacular sight. In the following days after the sinking, the ship's 64 cannon artillery was recovered, using the primitive diving systems at that time. Of the 64 cannons, 53 were sold to Germany in 1664. Nothing else could be recovered for the time being. The rest had to wait more than 300 years - until May, 1961, to be precise - to be salvaged from the bottom of the sea. This involved a great deal of work and considerable cost.

The fact that the ship had been found in surprisingly good condition, owing to the low salt levels of the Baltic Sea and its habitual low temperature (which prevents the action of the teredo or other underwater woodworm) facilitated a unique salvage operation that until this point in time was unique in history, besides costs that were hitherto unheard of.

At present, the ship, which has been completely restored, can be seen in the Wasa Museum in Stockholm.

Following pages, wheelhouse of the *Warrior.* Careful attention has been paid to every detail, even the most insignificant.

Carronade on board the Warrior. Note the grooves for the runners made of bronze across the teak deck.

45

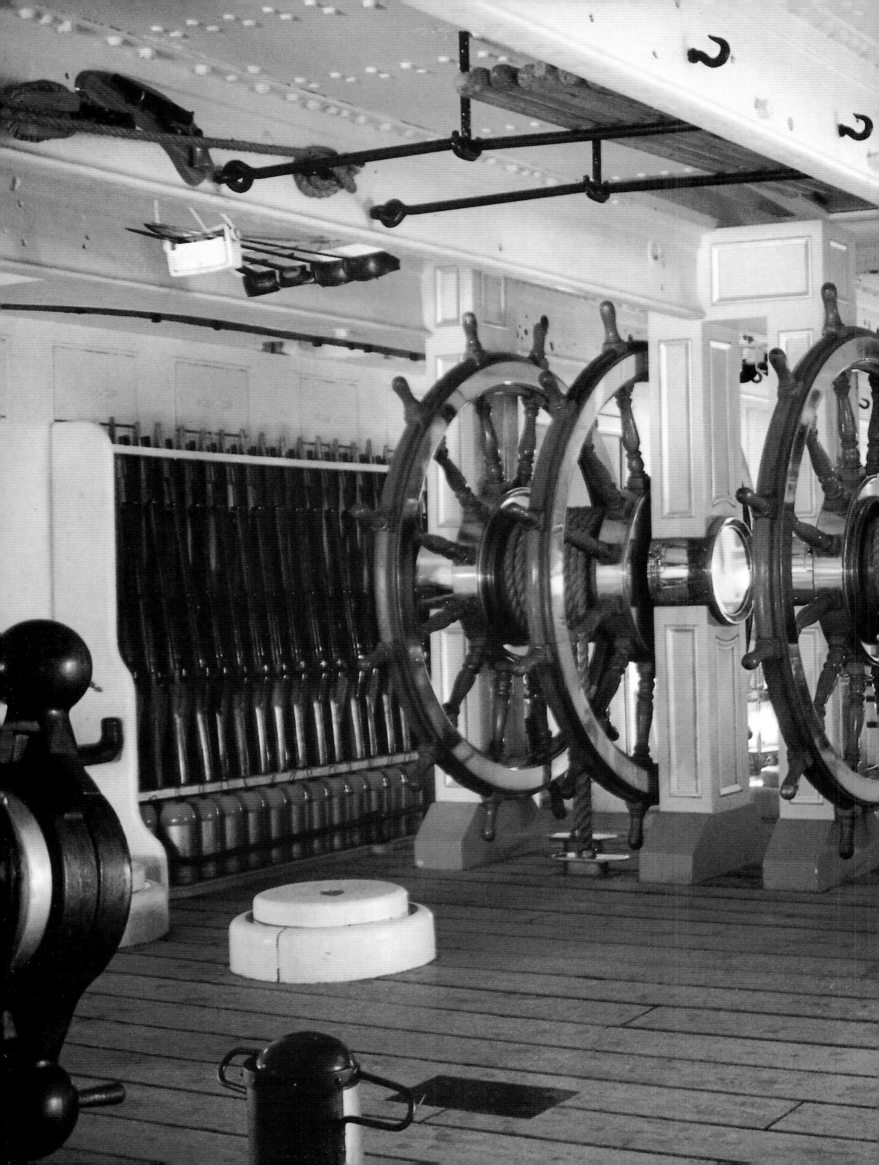

The ship of *Kyrenia*

In 1967 a Cypriot submarine crew member discovered the remains of a Greek cargo ship from the fourth century BC, near Kyrenia (Cyprus), at a depth of 98 feet, with a load of 30 tons and 49 feet in length. As the hull was found to be in good condition, it was possible to reconstruct 75 per cent quite accurately. Curiously its load of wine and almonds had been preserved for over more than 2,000 years under the sea.

In 1985 a sailable replica was built to carry out a complete study of its seaworthy qualities.

The galley *Marie-Rose* owes its construction to King Henry VIII himself and his wishes to increase the navy handed down to him by his father, ordering in 1509 the construction of two twin ships, the *Marie-Rose* and the *Peter Pomegranate*.

The *Marie-Rose* turned out to be a lucky and successful ship, so much so that it was highly praised by Sir Edward Howard, who used it as his flagship in the campaign against France.

In 1514, once the war with France had finished, its stay in the reserve fleet was used to make improvements and restructure its artillery by adding seven bronze cannons and another thirty-four made of iron, probably making it the most powerfully armed ship of the whole English fleet. In 1536 it was rebuilt, its displacement increased to 700 tons and armed with new bronze cannons. It sunk in 1545 during a confrontation with the French, near Portsmouth (about two miles away), in depths of 49 feet of water. Very few men survived.

The outstanding recovery work of the *Wasa* led to thoughts of the possible recovery of the *Marie-Rose*. The circumstances and the state of preservation were not the same, but it was worth trying to recover the buried part of the hull. In 1965 restitution work started and a committee was formed for its recovery in 1967. Between then and 1979, a great deal of exploration work was carried out, and in the same year a trust was created - of which Prince Charles is a member - for the recovery of the remains.

After much exploration it was confirmed that a large part of the hull that lay completely buried in the seabed had been conserved, and was worth recovering. However, being made of wood that had been buried in silt and mud for several centuries, its extraction was far from easy, as it fell apart upon handling. Excavation carried on until the remains of the hull had been completely uncovered. It was held up with cables attached to a metal structure, with these transporting it onto another metal frame, which brought it up to the surface and took it to the site that had been set up for it: dry dock number 3, neighbouring another celebrity ship, Nelson's *Victory*, in the naval base of Portsmouth.

Conserving that historical relic demanded a closed, complex installation, as it needed an atmosphere with a constant temperature of seven degrees and with humidity degrees higher than 90 per cent. Therefore water was sprayed at a certain temperature for 20 hours a day. In a few years time, when the wood has dried, plastic polymer is set to be injected into it, hardening and preven-

Pilot boat Tho-pa-ga (ex Tres Hermanos; ex Cala Tuent) and later *Espe-ran-ce,* moored in the wharf at Bosc i Alsina, Barcelona. It was built in Águilas (Murcia) in 1924, for Spanish ship owners. Unfortunately it was passed on to foreign owners as not one Spaniard was able to save it from being scrapped.

ting it from having to be constantly immersed in a damp atmosphere.

The hull of the *Marie-Rose* is exhibited in the historical area of Portsmouth's naval base, having been made into an audio visual museum, with an atmosphere that takes the visitor back to the period. It is difficult to calculate the cost of the rescue operation, but it is evident that it was considerable, as is its maintenance.

The work was carried out during the more favourable seasons of the years between 1965 and 1982, with the voluntary collaboration of a large number of workers, and sponsorship by several companies and official British institutions. Purely as an example, it should be pointed out that there were more than 600 volunteer divers who willingly offered their help without any financial gain.

Preservation of existing ships

Not all relics of the past that mankind possesses were obtained through such effort. There are some which only called out for a certain desire for preservation, a love of their own environment and to stand firm against commercial criteria that recommended they simply be sold as scrap. Something which is neither common, nor it would seem, easy, at least judging by certain experiences or specific cases.

There are quite a few countries that preserve ships that are an important part of their history. There is no room for differences here between those that developed a labour of a purely commercial nature or others that, in contrast, owe their recognition to battles. Likewise, in spite of there being many with mechanical propulsion, there are also sailing ships that have been saved from the passing of time, its ailments, or simply, from the voracity of the blowtorch. In this sense, it is reassuring to be able to confirm that there are those who continue to consider that "the ships of today will be the history of tomorrow", and that therefore it is good to see what we have today being conserved, and by doing so hoping to avoid future reconstruction or recovery at much greater expense.

Without meaning to concede that it is exclusive to English speaking countries, as there are others that have also managed to hold on to an important part of their maritime heritage, it has to be said that these countries *do* conserve many well known ships, a silent testimony to their love of the sea and what it has represented in their respective histories. Evidence of this are the ships with hull and iron masts, as well as those from the early times of steam such as the *Warrior,* and even true sailing ships that took part in the glorious chapters of sailing, such as the *Cutty Sark,* which can be seen and visited in many cities, ports, museums and moorings.

The *Victory,* a ship with three bridges, Admiral Horatio Nelson's flagship at Trafalgar; the *Cutty Sark,* famous clipper of the tea trade, immortalized by its battle with the *Thermopylae;* the *Constitution,* a North American frigate with 44 cannons, from the end of the eighteenth century; the *Constellation,* a corvette from the North American civil war; the *Warrior,* with frigate rigging and the first battleship of a long series that

Pilot boat Tho-pa-ga sets sail from Barcelona port to embark on a short charter cruise. For some time it was rented out in the Caribbean as a cargo ship for coastal trade.

Pilot boat Tho-pa-ga. Mainmast, deck and sheet detail from spanker boom jib.

Pilot boat Tho-pa-ga. Forecastle, bowsprit, hawsepipe, and anchor with its davit.

belonged to the Royal Navy; the *Charles W. Morgan*, a whaleboat that survived a long career; the *Discovery,* a brave and daring explorer of the polar seas and so on, and an extensive list of ships that can be visited and enable one to see how they revolutionised naval architecture and technology over the years. But not all these ships came to carry out the peaceful, educational roles they do today easily or silently. Many only got there after putting up a fight of titanic proportions in order to avoid a cruel destiny. Just as an example we will look at three such cases.

The *Cutty Sark*

The *Cutty Sark*, a ship constructed from a mixture of iron and wood, designed by Hercules Linton and launched in Dumbarton in 1869, started its brilliant life as a tea clipper, later it carried wool and was then sold to a Portuguese ship owner at the end of the century. Its rigging having been replaced with that of brigantine-schooner, it sailed

until 1922 when it was acquired by a captain named Dowman who restored it, returning it to its original frigate appearance. After his death in 1936, it was used as a training ship until 1949 and finally, in 1954, it was installed permanently at its current site in a dry dock of the Maritime Museum, in Greenwich near London.

The *Warrior*

A veteran fighter, the *Warrior* also had to struggle to reach its present situation. Launched on 29th December, 1860, it was the English answer to the French frigate *Gloire*, the first battleship in history that had recently been put into service. The *Warrior* surpassed the *Gloire* in artillery power, displacement and dimensions, becoming in its day the most powerful warship in the world, although soon after it became out-dated with the rapid progress of technology. The towering battleship emerged from the American Civil War, at the same time as warships such as the *Monitor* and

The meticulous detail of the cabins on the Sea Cloud. After the end of the Second World War, this ship was the yacht of the Dominican *Generalissimo* Rafael Trujillo and as such was renamed *Patria*.

Interior of the bridge of the Sea Cloud. During the Second World War, the millionaire Hutton gave it over to the US Navy who used it as a meteorological ship.

The dining room of the Sea Cloud. With a perfect and very authentic atmosphere. A few years after being abandoned in Central America, the ship was acquired by a German shipping company who used it for luxury charter.

An inviting and peaceful corner of the Sea Cloud. In a corridor that leads to the accommodation below the deck.

The deck of the Sea Cloud from the bow. Note the ship's masting and all the rigging. This ship with frigate rigging started its life as a yacht belonging to the North American millionaire Hutton.

the Swedish *Ericsson*, shortly followed by the *Devastation*, in 1871, the first battleship without masts or sails, leaving the *Warrior* totally obsolete.

On 14th May, it sailed under its own steam for the last time, docking at Portsmouth, where it took on a whole range of activities. In 1902 it became a torpedo vessel, going on to form part of the *Vernon* torpedo school, mooring as *Vernon III* in Porchester Creek. In 1923 it was withdrawn, intended to be sold, but no buyers were found. As the hull was in excellent condition, in 1929 it was towed to Milford Haven to be used as a floating fuel tank-jetty in Pembroke Dock, remaining as such until 1976. As the idea of its possible restoration had been considered since 1967, the corresponding foundation was established.

In 1979 it was towed to Hartlepool, where on inspection it was seen that the task of restoring the hull was greater than had at first appeared. It was difficult to know whether this could be achieved within the estimated budget of between £4 - 8 mi-

llion, as not only was there the corresponding cleaning work but also a great deal of skill, dexterity, taste and a thorough knowledge of the subject was required, and this was by no means easy to find some hundred years after its construction. Finally, nearly 60 years after its ostracism, on 16th June, 1987, it was received by the waters of Portsmouth with full honours. It is still there today as a floating exhibit, totally restored, both inside and out.

The *Galatea*, ex-*Clara Stella*, ex-*Glenlee*

In spite of Spain's long history of the subject, there are no sailing ships of great importance on exhibition. The only one that could have been shown was passed on to the English. This was the *Galatea*, a training ship belonging to the navy, whose sad story is worth telling if only to ensure that it never happens again.

In 1896 it was launched from the Scottish shipyard of Rodger & Co., construction number

Místico Rafael Verdera built in 1841, sailing in a classic ships regatta. One of the rare occasions in which the Spanish have been able to save a boat using their own means.

324. It had an iron hull and barrack rigging and carried the name of *Glenlee*.

It displaced around 2,700 tons and measured 246 feet in length and 39 in breadth, with a draught of more than 16. Its first owner was a shipping company made up of three partners who quickly sold it on to Ferguson & Co., another ship owner from Glasgow, who in turn sold it to the company Islamount Sailingship & Co., who renamed it the *Islamount*. Just before the Great War broke out it was sold to the British government who kept it in service until the war finished. Then it was sold again, this time to some Italian ship owners, who gave it the new name of *Clara Stella*.

In 1922 the Spanish navy acquired it and converted it into a seamanship school. It was bought for £20,000 of that time, to which another two million lira had to be added to satisfy the Triestine shipbuilder who repaired it and left it ready to set sail for Spain, where it was re-masted and had its two diesel engines checked along with the corresponding tailshafts.

After fitting out the living quarters - the change from cargo ship to school meant increasing its living space - it set off to carry out its first instruction cruise in 1926, a task that it continued until 1961. During this time it visited a great number of amicable ports and various countries, including Brazil, Cuba and the United States. It was a valiant ship with an excellent crew, demonstrated in the summer of 1957 when it went to the rescue of the four masted boat the *Pamir* and its crew, lost in the Atlantic in the middle of a violent storm with a great loss of young lives, as at the time it was a merchant training ship. No thought was given to the danger this rescue mission could entail, the *Pamir* being more modern by about ten years and considerably larger than the *Galatea*.

In 1959, the *Galatea* was immobilized in the navy yard at Ferrol as a pontoon-school, undergoing almost the last repair work on its hull in the dock at La Campana. With the arrival of the seventies, rumours started to circulate about possible scrapping being imminent, which wasn't helped by the fact that its hull was seen to be suffering from several leaks. By 1985, it could be seen moored, with its masts removed and lying across the dock in one of the jetties belonging to the Naval Station at La Graña, near Ferrol. At that time various Spanish cities and museums started to show an interest in the ship, finally obtaining bits and pieces such as part of the furniture that was given to the Barcelona Maritime Museum. Several options were considered - some truly outlandish like the talk of dividing it two, transporting it by road to Madrid where the two halves would be rejoined and then set afloat on the lake in the Casa de Campo - but none of these were ever put into action.

Finally, after having been chosen in the competition with other Spanish cities, the Spanish Navy handed the ship over to Seville, first spending a large part of its budget on making it seaworthy enough to reach the city. It was towed there by the tugs *Punta Roca* and *Montgó*. With adequate funds at its disposal, the San Telmo Trust, which nearly all the institutions and bodies of the city belonged to, committed itself to restoring the ship and keeping it on display in the Andalusian capital, mooring it to one of its piers and including it as one of the key pieces in the 1992 Universal Exhibition.

However, in the end the project was scrapped. With neither Andalusian sponsors nor institutions, after having appeared in the photo, continuing to show interest in the ship, which ran aground on the shore at El Guadalquivir, close to the Sevillian company Españoles Shipyard, plc. As time went by it became a refuge for the homeless and drug addicts who, in an attempt to keep warm, set a fire going with the little wood that remained. Firemen put out the fire and in doing so caused it to sink at a shallow depth, leaving it protruding from the water. At the beginning of 1990, seeing the derelict state it had ended up in, it was suggested the navy recuperate and scrap it at their expense.

For a while scrapping the ship was again seriously considered, but as the cost of carrying this out was quite a lot higher than the materials were actually worth, the idea was abandoned, and besides, nobody any longer had any interest in the project. Finally, at the beginning of 1992, the Spanish navy - who had meanwhile recovered its property – tried to sell the ship at a public auction (26th February, 5 million pesetas; 30th March the price was dropped) with the end result of neither parties benefiting. At the last moment, luck arrived to help the tired, battered, ill-fated ship in the form of The Clyde Maritime Trust Co., a British maritime institution that showed interest in its acquisition for a symbolic amount and in whose country it can currently be found in the stages of restoration.

El Boleh sailing with the spinnaker hoisted, during one of the legs of the 9th Trophy "Almirante Conde de Barcelona".
Right, brig-schooner Atlantis. Another ship saved from being scrapped and currently used for charter voyages.

Balandro 15M International Tuiga viewed from the bow sailing close haul. This is a regatta ship for top competition, built in England in 1908, in the charge of Duke of Medinacelli. *Right, the Bla Jungfrun*, a beautiful schooner with two masts built in 1895, with classical rigging (two masts with spanker sails and flying jibs) and almost 78 feet in length.

Ketch Arosa, one of the sports boats belonging to the Spanish Navy, built in 1931, lowering the spinnaker to take a buoy. *Right, El Scipio,* a wonderful little sailing boat rigged with spanker, topsail and flying jibs, built in 1928, under English ownership.

Ketch Mingary, spectacular sports boat from the most elegant years of sailing (1929), detail that shows off the lines of its hull and sail rigging.

The rigging of the Tuiga showing topsail detail. These boats are made entirely of wood, with cotton sails and hemp ropes, added to this the cost of the crew they are very expensive and maintenance is reserved only for special cases.

PART III
Style Ships

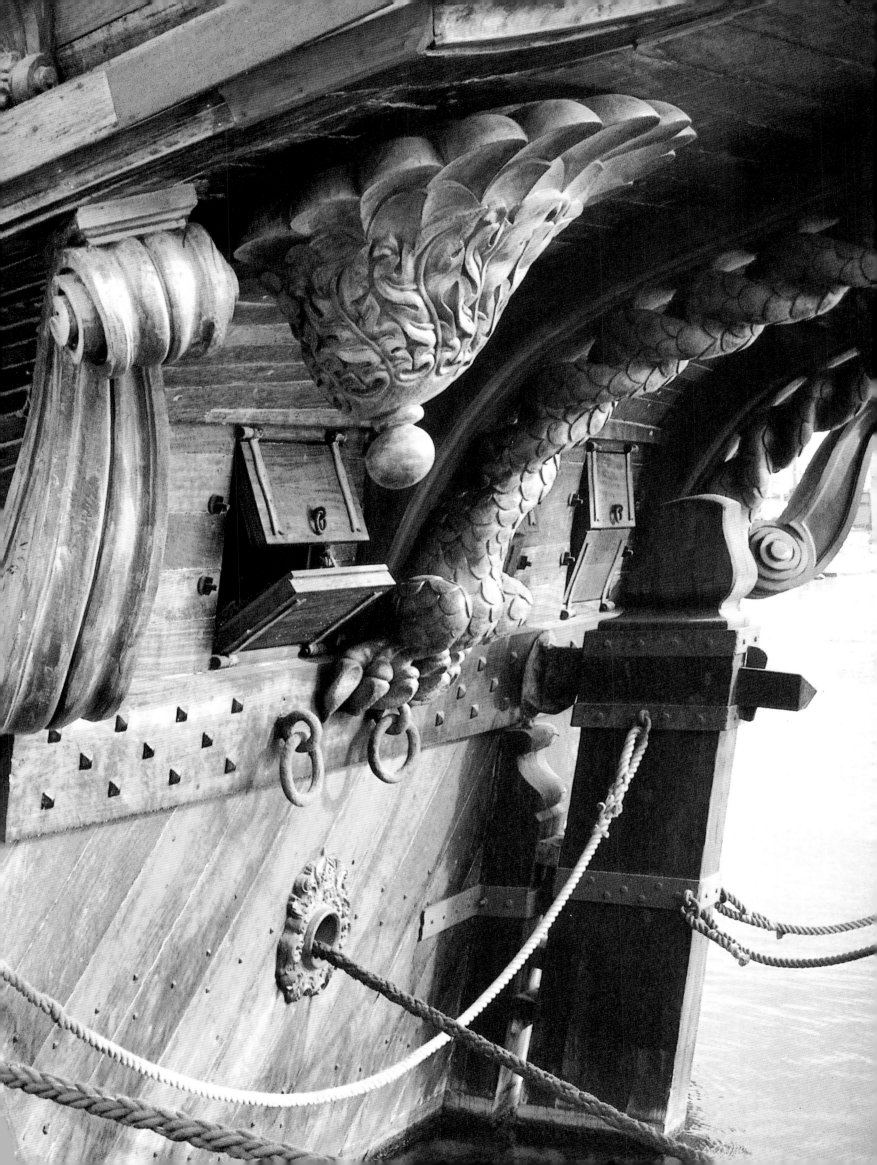

Cross section of a 74 cannon ship, viewed from in front of the mizzen mast and from bow to stern. Note how the water outflow from the stern gives the hull a conical line below the flotation line reducing useful spaces. The central column is the well of the bilge pumps, with a suspended lantern. The square openings above the bulkhead at the back covered by sliding partitions close off the room where bread and biscuits are stored. On the artillery deck, with two open portholes, and behind the ladder are the armouries with firearms and shackles. The officers' chambers and dining room are located behind the bulkhead of the first deck. The small windows of the bulkhead on the upper deck are to the officers' quarters and the door at the port leads to that of the first lieutenant. On the outside of the hull and behind the mizzen chain wales, the stern balconies' row structure.

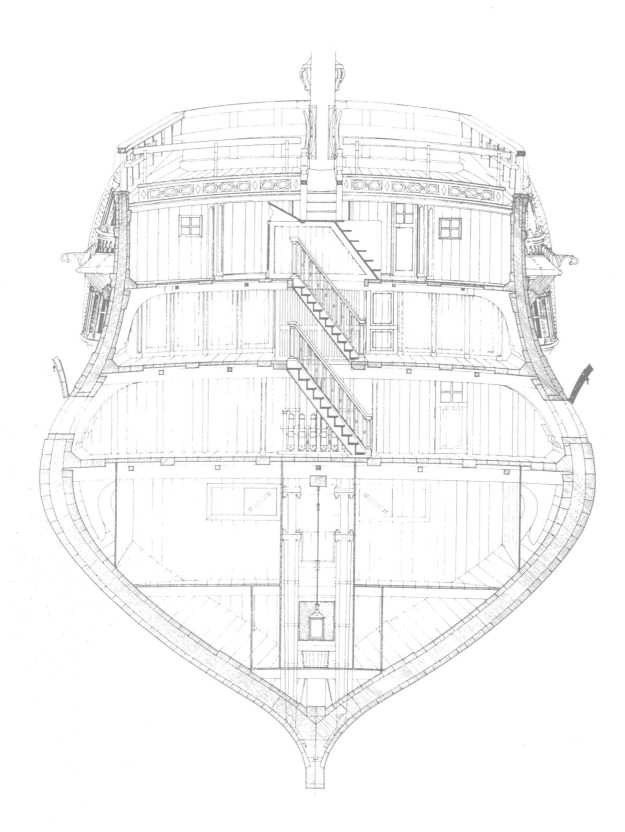

Cross section of a 74 cannon ship, viewed from in front of the main mast, from bow to stern, at the height of the bilge pumps chamber. The hold carries ballast and several rows of barrels containing different cargo, anything from flour to salted provisions or wood for the kitchen stove. The pipes of the central well go as far as the first deck, with the bilge pumps situated on both sides of the main mast. On the living quarters deck, provisions were loaded into different compartments of which some partitions, bulkheads and door handles can be seen. The bridge or artillery deck shows the back of the gun room bulkhead, with the access door next to the port. The dotted line above the first deck and that which covers the bilge pumps indicates the position of the boats and skiffs of the ship. The two round pieces seen from above on this deck are the topgallant masts. The poop deck shows the access to the chambers, in front of which are the main mast and the bell above the gunwale; in the same space as the bell there would often be a bottle of sand. The upper deck fills the top half of the picture. The masts' chain wales are situated on the outside of the hull.

Cross section of a 74 cannon ship, viewed from behind the foresail mast and from the stern to the bow. Between the plan and the hold is the ballast. Above the deck of the hold the coiled hawsers are visible, between both coils those of the anchor, and above that of the living compartment other lines also coiled. In the centre of the artillery deck, a deck hatch can be seen and behind this is the water crate, above the bulkhead at the back the two hawsepipes can be seen. The octagonal pieces which are above the first deck are topmasts seen from above and the bulkhead between the two ladders with a cross is the kitchen. On the forecastle deck are the pin rails from the foot of the foresail, with the gunwale and the bell. On the outside of the hull, at the same level as the deck, the chain wales can be seen with the deadeyes lowered and the chainplates.

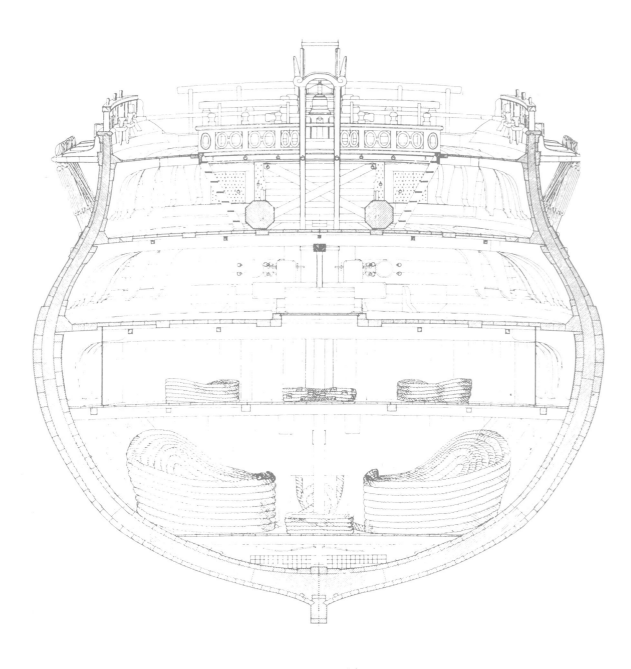

According to the old proverb, "All that glitters is not gold" and a lot of the time this is true. In recent years a few old ships have been built which are really outstanding to look at, but whose age is not what it seems. They are known as 'style ships'.

These ships are built using plans and original documentation and only materials considered "classical" can be used in their construction.

However, this rule is not always kept to, at least in cases where the final appearance is all important. So when we are looking at a particular ship, unless we have some knowledge on the subject, it is very difficult to ascertain whether it is a 'style ship' or not. But in any case, it is quite likely that in our eyes this will be of little importance as we are more interested in the spectacular impression we are left with.

Among the different 'style' ships that can be seen, three particularly catch the viewer's attention. They are a galleon, whose appearance recalls the Elizabethans of the sixteenth and seventeenth centuries; a ship with three bridges, possibly dating back to the seventeenth or early eighteenth century, and a ship that is of a much more recent age, though still very fine in appearance, a topsail schooner from the end of the nineteenth century.

The galleon: king of the seas

The galleon is a ship that could be said to be in transition and therefore difficult to define. It is often referred to as a link in the chain that led the evolution from the carrack and the nao, among others, to the ship. There is no total unanimity of criteria, and opinions differ regarding the name's origin. There are those who think it was applied more to a ship that performed a specific task rather than a particular type of ship itself. But there are also those who consider that 'galleon' is a word that comes from galley, indicating that it concerned a ship with greater length-breadth relation - meaning a greater extension ratio - with less bilge than ordinary ships and so lighter and easier to handle; hence the name was applied to ships that met these requirements.

But it should also be remembered that at this time (sixteenth century), quite often galleon generically referred to all powerful warships with great displacement, without even considering hull lines or rigging. Tying in with this is the existence of ships called galleons conform to this model (like the *galleon of Venice*, a ship with vast displacement, excessively large armament and terrible stability, that consequently sank in 1569 at its anchorage in Malamocco after a heavy shower, when it heeled quickly and capsized) even though their construction characteristics do not. Also in France, during King Francis I's reign, certain ships were known as galleons (galleasses built in Le Havre) and later, by now in the times of Cardinal Richelieu, a craftsman and the driving force behind the modern French navy, all ships of the time (seventeenth and eighteenth century) were known as galleons. In England, during Queen Elizabeth I's reign, 'galleon' was the name given to seamen and not boats, although naval architecture talks of Elizabethan galleons as well as Spanish and Flemish. Lastly, in Spain at around the time of the discovery of America, all ships that traded with America, bringing riches from the Indies to the Peninsula, were also generically named galleons, in particular the ship that between 1571 and 1734, exclusively covered the route between the American continent and the Philippines, the 'Galeón de Manila'. It is very interesting and illustrative, in this aspect, that the same ship was also known as the 'Nao de la China' even though it was evidently in no way related to that type of ship.

There nevertheless seems to be certain agreement in considering the galleon as a type of ship, longer and narrower than the nao, although shorter and wider proportionately than the galley, and as was indicated earlier, formed the transition of the caravel and the nao to the ship. It reached its zenith in the sixteenth century when it became the Spanish ship of the Atlantic, as it was evident that the ships of the discovery, naos and caravels - and on a smaller scale the galleys and the galleasses - were not suited to long ocean voyages. Their rigging, in general, consisted of three or four masts with square sails (foresail and main) and lateen (mizzen and mizzen topgallant) to which was added the bowsprit (spritsail) and often armed with a storm rig (outer spritsail).

The galleons were ships without oars - even though there are prints that show otherwise - with high forecastles and even longer, excessively ornate and high poop decks and quarterdecks, with two or more decks, all very richly ornamented. Their displacement was often very great - the *San*

the flotation line - a consequence of the special features needed for river navigation as cities that were further inland such as Seville and Bruges needed to be reached, resulting in a minimal draught, potbellied bilge and high upper works. Its ornamentation was very abundant and excessive, quite often with religious motifs, which in time became so baroque in style and sumptuousness that laws had to be introduced to limit its extent, especially on captains' ships. Laws were not always complied with, particularly in cases where the admirals enjoyed a high social position or had great wealth at their disposal, with which they often paid the ship's expenses in order to keep up the level of luxury they felt obliged to maintain.

Several names remain linked to the galleon, such as *Flota de la Tierra Firme; Nueva España; Guarda de la Carrera de Indias* or others more related to places, like *Acapulco* and *Peru.*

The *Every*

To come across a pirate galleon in the middle of the twentieth century would seem unlikely, but even more incredible that such a galleon exists and is the work and dream of an impassioned fan who has built it with his own hands, starting off with a minesweeper from the Second World War, and helped at weekends by a few friends. And despite everything this is exactly what happened. In around 1940, in one of the many minor shipyards that proliferated in the firths of Scotland, where there is an inheritance of traditions that made English naval carpenters so famous, a small minesweeper was built with a wooden hull, the MMS-265 (Motor Minesweeper), a robustly built ship with a squat appearance, particularly suitable for the tasks it would have to perform. It had a displacement of 165 tons, a length of more than 118 feet, a breadth of seven and a draught of less than three. Propelled by a 500 horsepower diesel motor, it reached speeds of 11 knots. It carried a twenty-man crew and was armed with two 12.7 machine guns in a double frame, as well as several complete dredging facilities.

Having survived the war it was demilitarized, being sold along with many others to private ship owners. In 1947 a Norwegian ship owner renamed it the *Every* and registered it in Narvik. Dedicated for 30 years to coastal merchant shipping around

Martín of 1582 reached 1,200 tons, although there were others that just scraped 500. Particularly famous were the *Doce Apóstles,* twelve identical galleons that left Seville twice a year and returned to Spain laden with riches. So valuable in fact was the load a galleon usually carried that, with the aim of changing its master, powerful ships or corsairs, if not simple pirate ships, would be ready and waiting. This pillaging instigated the invention of convoys, in which a fleet of merchant galleons sailed protected by another similar fleet that was more powerfully armed and equipped for war, or at least enough to see off any attackers.

One very characteristic feature of this type of ship was the 'violin stern' as it was called - a gradual reduction in the breadth of the decks above the ports of the surrounding seas, it did not seem at that time that such a ship could harbour thoughts about greater companies. In 1977 it changed hands, being acquired by a German merchant seaman, Captain Volker Köhne, who poured all his passion for ships and patrimony into her.

For the next five years he worked tirelessly on his project, determined to convert it into a close resemblance of an Elizabethan galleon, a task in which a chosen group of friends participated and who offered whatever they could: time, money... and even their own families, as the captain and his wife had recently separated. The workload was much greater than had at first appeared. The cabin, deck and original beams all had to be dismantled as the forecastle needed to be well supported and the long masts had to cross all the decks until resting on the keel mast keelsons. The initial budget soon appeared unrealistic and was surpassed which was why a bar was installed in the forecastle in order to repair the injured treasury a little. Finally, one bright and memorable day in 1983, more than five and a half years after the start of the project, work was finished.

By the spring of 1983, once all the bureaucratic obstacles had been overcome, the ship was declared fit to sail and started off on its travels. It began with short trips to Kiel and Lübeck and on one such voyage reached Copenhagen. Later a relationship was established with the children's association SOS. An agreement was soon reached and the ship became an official collaborator. When it had been thoroughly tested out and judged reasonably safe to sail, the idea of a round the world trip started to be considered. The first ports were all the important ones in the North Sea, the coasts of the Channel, Brittany, the Bay of Biscay and then along the Cantabrian coast, stopping off at all ports. Next it sailed to Galicia, Portugal and the provinces in south st Spain. It reached the Mediterranean and st ced to sail up the Spanish coast. A violent storm took it by surprise at Cape Palos causing serious damage in the oarlock of the propeller shaft. On reaching Cartagena and mooring in its dock it sank but was refloated, provisionally repaired and continued on its way. Then it arrived in Barcelona where it spent the Christmas of 1984, staying for three months' rest and repair.

It left Barcelona in March, 1985, heading for the south of France, and once again it came up against a violent storm, with force 9 gales and wa-

ves more than 32 feet high, damaging its masts and forcing it to seek refuge in Mahón (the best ports in the Mediterranean are said to be July, August and Mahón). It briefly returned to Barcelona for a general check and then took up its voyage once again, heading for the ports of the south of France, the Italian peninsula and the Dalmatian coast, finally reaching Greece and Turkey.

It was planned to take the route up the Suez Canal towards Arabia, Yemen, Oman, western Pakistan, India, Ceylon, Malaysia, Indonesia and Australia. In spite of it being said to have sailed all the way to Sydney, where it would appear to have arrived at the end of 1991, or the beginning of 1992, this cannot be confirmed, and it is feared that it got caught up in the Kuwait conflict - Summer 1990 - and has not been heard of since.

The Every entering the deponent and floating dock of Barcelona – also now non-existent and broken up – for careening and repair work.

View of the stern of
The Every .

The Every seen from clo-sed stern.

Starboard foresail chain wales on galleon *Every*, as well as its set of deadeyes and lanyards.

Part of the decks and masting of the *Every*, from the poop deck.

The ship of the line: sovereign among sovereigns

Until some time into the sixteenth century there are no notable differences between what we call today 'merchant ships' and 'warships'. Merchant ships were required to be armed in order to defend themselves, at the same time as needing some of the most common characteristics to the so-called 'warship' (mobility, manoeuvrability, etc.) but the only difference between them was quite minimal, if they sailed in the name of the crown they were 'warships' but if it was for their own benefit they were 'merchants'; although they could never really claim to be independent.

The fact that the galleons were armed and grouped together in convoys meant that larger ships, with a greater and more powerful artillery were needed in order to ward off their attackers more efficiently. They consequently started to build ships with much greater displacement and artillery power than the galleons, whose use was limited to warfare. The first models were failures, with neither the French nor the English managing to produce a truly efficient ship until the *Great Harry* (better known as *Henry Grace a Dieu*) was introduced in 1536. Often thought to be the first real 'ship', although there are those who would describe it as a carrack with eight decks, eight masts (jib, main, mizzen and mizzen topgallant); it is considered the first ship that used masts consisting of more than one piece.

Strictly speaking, construction work on the *Great Harry* started on 3rd October, 1512 and was launched in 1514. The ship was ordered by King Henry VIII himself and in its time was the largest fleet ship in existence as it had a displacement of about 1,000 tons. Its first armament was 184 cannons (136 culverins and 48 large-calibre guns), later reduced to 122 in around 1536, completed with hand armament - which today would be considered as personal arms - which totalled 500 yew longbows, 120 string bows, 200 pikes, 200 boarding axes and a great number of arrows and lances. It is evident that two centuries after the arrival of gunpowder on board ships (*La Rochela*, 1371), weapons such as knives and swords continued to be used on board.

The *Great Harry* was destroyed in 1553 by fire and so did not take part in the battle that took place in 1558, the destruction of the Great Armada, unfortunately named The Invincible, in which it started to become clear that a longer range, faster shooting artillery was a definite advantage. This battle, to a greater or lesser extent, marked the end

Every forecastle deck, above the back of the quarterdeck and forecastle. In the foreground the foresail mast and its pin rails at the foot of the mast.

Cannon held in position according to state of the sea (in this drawing, for calm seas) or port. In the drawing a part of the rigging has been omitted (a block secured to the ring of the gun carriage which works with two eye block and tackle) for greater clarity. The verification of the effectiveness of lifting each piece corresponded to the constable or the ropes of the cannon.

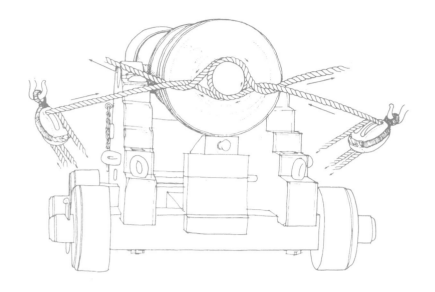

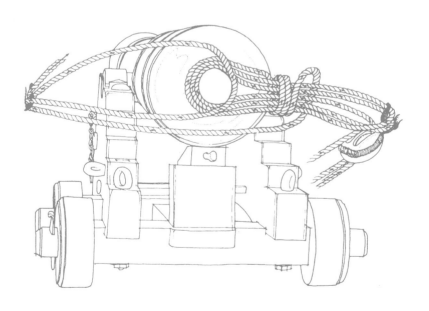

Cannon held in position according to the state of sea (in this drawing, for stormy seas). A part of one rigging has been omitted as well as another almost complete rigging for greater clarity in the drawing. The block that corresponds to the right block and tackle and almost all of the rigging on the left. This type of cannon support was needed when bad seas were forecast. A lowered cannon could be extremely dangerous as its weight and inertia devastated anything that should happen to be in front of it. This was, until something or someone put an end to its mad journey across the deck, or else it would end up rolling over board, although not before smashing and making a large hole in it.

of boarding in attack, apart from that climax of naval combat of the time (it is said that the battle of Lepanto in 1571 was just like a battle of infantry but fought out on galleys) which later remained reserved for very specific occasions.

There was very little evolution of the ship until the middle of the following century in which the appearance of the English *Sovereign of the Seas* (1637) and the French *La Couronne* (1638) started to mark a slight but nonetheless significant change. The former is said to have displaced more than 1,600 tons and for a long time was considered the first three-deck ship (the first in fact was the *Prince Royal,* 1610); the hull continued to maintain its towering and striking stern superstructure (poop deck and quarterdeck), although it lost its high forecastle. Its rigging kept the four customary masts, but with one necessary change brought about by the need to improve evolutionary ability and forward tacking: the square sail of the mizzen above the mast of the lateen. The French *La Couronne* slightly lowered the height of the top of the stern and reduced the number of masts, from four to three and removed the mizzen topgallant. In this way a bigger mizzen was used and changed to using a lateen sail with a greater surface (adding up to that of the mizzen topgallant) and added a good sized square sail. Its displacement was 1,000 tons, substantially greater than other similar ships which scarcely reached 500.

There is a story concerning *La Couronne* which could perhaps be considered as one of the earliest claims for the defence of ecology, something particularly relevant today. In order to build *La Couronne,* which took ten years, a whole wood belonging to the duke of Rohan was cut down, which infuriated the duchess as she considered it a disproportionate amount for one boat.

The successive improvements applied to the ship concern the development of the water outflow of the hull - which improved manoeuvrability by enabling greater effectiveness of the rudder and not the transom - followed by the appearance of studding sails in the seventeenth century; flying jibs in the second half of seventeenth and beginning of eighteenth century; the staysail and the spanker sail in the second half of the eighteenth century.

The appearance of the spanker sail deserves special attention. It is said that around 1750 an English captain, who had suffered a split in the

bow part of the lateen mast of the mizzen, cut the part of the bow sail that was left over and secured it to the mast. The result was so successful that he decided to go ahead with the innovation. Some time later all ships carried a spanker sail instead of a lateen, but with the mizzen yard complete – meaning that one part stood out sharply at the bow from the mizzen mast – a feature that lasted for quite some time.

For more than two whole centuries - seventeenth, eighteenth and part of the nineteenth - the ship of the line, so called for the lines it formed when in battle, was the undisputable and undisputed sovereign of the fighting fleets, reaching well-known degrees of perfection in design and function.

Main decks, of the quarterdeck and poop deck of the ship *Neptuno* viewed from the castle.

73

The arrival of the steam ship and modern artillery marked the decline of the sailing ship, the Battle of Trafalgar 21st October, 1805, possibly considered its swan song. This decline became even clearer when the first tests of the Paixhan cannon with explosive grenades were carried out in Brest in 1822 on the old ship *Pacificator*. The ship was totally wrecked during the disaster in Sinope, Turkey on 30th November, 1853, in which more than 2,000 Turks lost their lives and which triggered the end of the wooden ship, the Crimean War and the appearance of the battle-ship.

The *Neptuno*

There are quite a few ships of all kinds that have been built for use as film sets. We have already seen that of one of the reproductions of the caravel *Santa María* was created for the filming of "Alba de América". But in the 1980s when the possibility arose of constructing a complete seventeenth century ship for the filming of "Pirates" by Roman Polanski, one person threw their hands up to their head.

There was certain controversy concerning the type of ship that the *Neptuno* was. It is said that for its design and construction, the French decorator Pierre Guffroy accumulated a great deal of information about Spanish galleons. But as certain characteristics of the ship (displacement, rigging, shape of the hull, absence of a high forecastle, etc) mean it is more like a seventeenth century ship than a galleon of the sixteenth century, we will describe it as the former and not the latter. As mentioned earlier there is plenty of confusion about both types of ships and their names. All of which being said with the pertinent reservations as there may be those who differ in opinion and think the opposite.

The *Neptuno* is a ship with mechanical propulsion (two Schottel propellers, or active rudders of 400 horsepower giving it a maximum speed of 5 knots), whose rigging is purely decorative, although it has to be strong enough to support the sails, and in some way, keep them billowing so that it looks like they propel the ship. Notwithstanding this, it is still a true ship capable of making limited voyages. Its mainly iron structure is covered with decorative materials such as wood (solid or plywood) or ornamentation (carving, figures, artillery, etc.) made of fibreglass. In the strictest sense it should not be considered a 'style ship', as it uses materials that are strictly prohibited. It is included here for no other reason than that it is a nautical rarity and its presence, independent of the materials used in its construction, is superb.

Capstan on the main deck of the Neptuno. In the background, the castle with foresail mast. And at the end, the bowsprit and spritsail yard.

Detail of the Castile and Leon Shield which, on the gunwale of the quarterdeck, presides over the main deck of the *Neptuno*.

General view of the Neptuno from the stern and the fashion piece of the starboard.
Note how the main mast is broken at the topsail, and also the general bad state of the sails and rigging, as a consequence of battling through a violent storm.

Detail of the *Neptuno* seen from its port side.

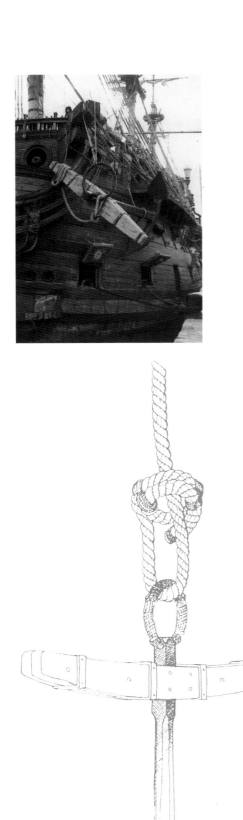

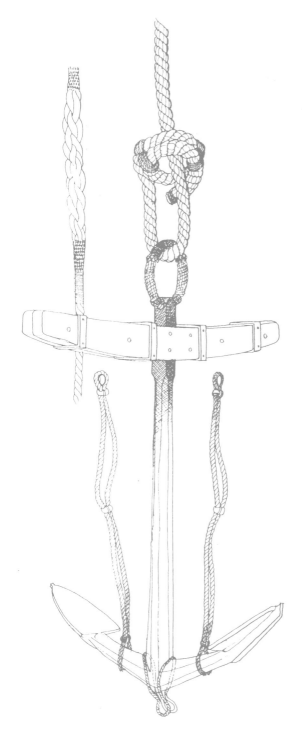

Heavy anchors from a 74 cannon ship with their clinches and rigging. Left, common bower anchor (with wooden stocks) clinched, showing detail of the clinch. *Right,* stocks anchor (wooden stocks) clinched, again showing clinch detail, with rigging for releasing it from the bottom; anchor arm, fluke or crown. With the aid of these, the anchor could be released from the bottom when it was firmly gripped. Pulling at them enabled one to loosen them from the bottom, once it had been released it could then be hoisted up normally.

Detail of the stern balconies on the Neptuno.
Small photo, detail of the projection of the stern, decoration and rudder. From the rudder's arrangement (without a tiller passing across the transom) and chain wales, it is clear that it cannot actually work in manoeuvring.

The building of the ship, carried out in Bizerta, Malta and Tunisia, lasted two whole years (April 1984 to May 1986). It displaces 1,500 tons and measures 203 feet in total length and 54 in breadth. The final cost was more than 8 million dollars, although it was insured by Lloyds of London for $30 in order to cover any possible damage caused in the filming, with the foreseeable losses.

Once the filming was over, it sailed unaided to Cannes for the 39th Film Festival where it remained on show to promote the film. It also made 140 television appearances during the event. Later in 1987 it also sailed to Barcelona, where it stayed to have repair work done particularly on the hull and rigging which had been damaged in a storm.

A controversial matter: the nomenclature of sailing ships

It is not easy to classify the different types of sailing ships according to the particular characteristics of their rigging, in fact it is one of the most complicated aspects of nautical knowledge. On one hand there are a great number of sailing ships, many of them with mixed characteristics, which leads to the use of compound names to identify them more accurately (topsail schooner, fore-topsail schooner, brig-schooner, etc.), based on very subtle differences. On the other hand, names and classifications vary from place to place, maybe depending on a simple – or not, if you happen to be an expert - detail of the rigging, not always so visible or well-known, but still of great importance.

There are very specific types exclusive to particular countries or areas, with their own names that have become universalized, thus complicating the matter furthermore. This added to the habitual lack of knowledge of naval terms, plus the obvious jokes that aren't totally insincere ('why is a boat called round?' – 'because it has square sails') can end up putting people off the whole subject.

And if all this wasn't enough, a further problem arose, that of translation. When translating

The bow, stem and bowsprit of the Pride of Baltimore, seen in close up, with details of the chain wales and bowsprit.

very similar names that were sometimes abbreviated, which weren't always the same, terms became confused and concepts mixed up resulting in a mishmash of ideas verging on gobbledygook. Added to that the total lack of control in many circles, with the appearance of veritable atrocities in the eyes of someone with knowledge on the subject, the general confusion degenerated into technological apathy. For example: hoist the sheet - a sheet is not usually hoisted but sheeted - or "the ship has arrived in the port listed to port and starboard" (sic).

Semantics put the icing on the cake with its figures, and ended up foisting a name on that whose technical definition described it as something else. But for the sake of a better rhyme, metrics or any other grammatical convenience, it was allowed to stay (corvette instead of frigate, etc.), magnified by the corresponding illustration in which what one looked for was better aesthetics.

The end result is that of having to study encyclopaedias, technical dictionaries and specialized

General view of the topsail schooner of 1812, Pride of Baltimore, built between 1987 and 1988, by the shipbuilder G. Peter Boudreu, according to the naval architect Thomas C. Gillmer's plans.

Detail of the Pride of Baltimore's foresail base and adjacent parts. These ships' rigging consisted of a typical spanker stern line handler with a large surface, a long boom that stuck out from behind the transom.

Base of the main mast of the Pride of Baltimore showing its characteristic system of bending on the main sail, and the openings of the gaff on the boom and the peak of the main. Another detail is the boom support table at the base of the mast.

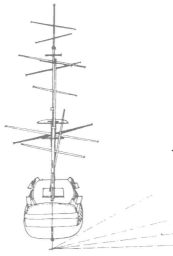

Rigging manoeuvre of a ship on setting sail.

The ship is anchored, bow to the wind, the anchor at the port with a good anchorage, without any obstacles. The particular position of the anchoring allows for a slight drift towards starboard (starboard leeward).

◄ **1.** The foresail yards wave in the direction of the port and those on the main and mizzen towards starboard, finishing up in opposite directions. The anchor capstan is then set to work.

2. The ship has dropped about two quarters to starboard, while the anchor has been let out until it is sunken. The topsails and topgallants of the main and mizzen flap can also be seen. On releasing the anchor the starboard drops further and the mizzen sail starts to work. ►

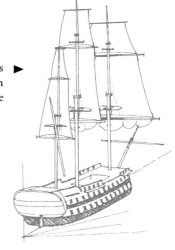

◄ **3.** A flying jib is hoisted and secured at port and the ship drops further towards starboard. The anchor is hoisted, and if it drops excessively towards one side or the other the mizzen sail is worked to compensate. The sails are kept in a lie to position and totally inactive. With this manoeuvre, four more quarters are gained from the wind.

5. With all the sails hoisted and directed to the wind, the ship just starting to steer towards its chosen route, the day's run starts with a clear 'full speed ahead'.

▼

▲

4. The sails start to be positioned and the boat drops another six quarters. The topsails and topgallants of the main and mizzen are now under the wind, whereas those of the foresail are not. The ship starts to pick up speed and steer. The anchor is raised up to the davits to which it is secured and held in place.

Side view of the Volchitsa. Its rigging can be seen very clearly: main and foresail with spankers and without topsails, royal sail and two good-sized jibs. Also note both masts are 'on end'.

The Volchitsa viewed from bow starboard. It can be seen that the masts only have two pieces (male and top mast), a detail which according to different opinions, does not allow it to qualify as a brig-schooner. *Right,* a detail of the chain wales, masting and jib sails, with the topsail loaded.

Schooner Volchitsa. Detail
of the hull: transom.

works in search of a particular definition or precise detail - something which is not always possible - which enables an unequivocal identification of a specific rig. And this is a task we all end up doing insofar as it is difficult to avoid error.

The *Volchitsa*, a Russian in the Mediterranean

In post-Gorbachev Russia at the end of the 1980s, a group of sea enthusiasts, one of them a naval engineer, embarked on a project of thorough research in the naval museums and shipyards in search of a ship that was relatively classical, a record of the age of sailing, attractive in appearance and which would be feasibly possible to reconstruct.

Finally they got hold of the plans of a topsail schooner from the end of the nineteenth century, a cabotage cargo ship from the Baltic Sea, embarking on the construction, carried out in the Petrodzavodsk shipyard on the banks of Lake Ladoga in 1992. It made its way to the Baltic via the river Neva and San Petersburg, the old Tsarist Petrograd or communist Leningrad, sailing next to another historical ship, the *Aurora*, the famous light cruiser from which the first shots were fired at the Winter Palace during the Russian Revolution in 1917.

The *Volchitsa*, registered in San Petersburg, displaces 64 tons and measures a length, between perpendiculars (from rudder turn axis to the flotation fore) of 57.7 feet and a maximum of 97.4 feet. At the end of the winter of 1992 it set off for warmer seas and in May was approaching the Straits of Gibraltar, where it received a warm welcome from a fleet of NATO warships that were carrying out exercises there and was honoured by the passing of the Spanish aircraft carrier *Principe de Asturias*.

Arriving in Barcelona at the beginning of that summer it made several charter voyages and later in August journeyed on to Majorca to take part in the 9th Classic Boats Trophy 'Almirante Conde de Barcelona' where it was awarded a prize. It sailed back to Barcelona in September and stayed there throughout autumn for repair and maintenance work, as a new propeller and general motor repair were required. At the beginning of 1994 it moved on to Santa Cruz, Tenerife with the intention of continuing its activity of discretionary holiday charter trips.

Following pages, the "Volchitsa" sailing near the Strait of Gibraltar.

On the deck, at the stern of the main mast and below the boom of the spanker sail: control panel for the machines ropes and chains that hold it fast.

Topsail Schooner Volchitsa.
Crosstree detail of the main and various work manoeuvres. *Below*, forecastle detail the hoisting windlass and the manoeuvre rigging.

The Lateen Sail

The sailboat known as the lateen, undoubtedly the most typical and used in the Mediterranean, did not become well known because of the Romans. Authors say its name comes from the corruption of the expression "a la trina" which referred to the shape of the boat itself, although some say the expression was pronounced by people from Nordic countries on arriving in the Mediterranean and seeing the boat for the first time.

However it came about, it became the most widely used sailboat in the Mediterranean and is the most representative of this sea. It is also presently considered the second oldest sailboat known to have existed (the first is the junk). It is believed to have originated in the Indian Ocean - or perhaps even further afield, from the Polynesian praos - and to have reached the Mediterranean across the Red Sea. The Byzantines are thought to be its first champions and the Arabs to have introduced it.

As a sailboat, it is particularly suitable for sailing close haul (against the wind), a type of sailing that is also known as 'sailing by the bowline' or 'beating to windward'. Due to this particular characteristic it continues to be used in limited spaces of water, where favourable winds do not always blow, as can be seen in the Red Sea or Persian Gulf. In diagonal winds and sailing close haul the lateen has no rival, although the square sail surpasses it when sailing downwind.

Closely linked to several Mediterranean ships (galley, xabeck, felucca, etc.), its golden age was between the twelfth and seventeenth centuries, although the xabecks carried this into the nineteenth century, the feluccas and other cabotage ships into the mid-twentieth century and even up to today; fishing boats (seiners, catboats, boulters, sardine boats, etc.). All of these have brought the lateen up to the present day, in which the internal combustion engine has left it permanently isolated from professional use. However, it is still used practically all over the Mediterranean, and on certain coasts for professional use. It is also enjoying a slight resurgence in terms of leisure, sport and festivities.

"La vida de la galera déla Dios a quien la quiera"(popular Spanish saying)

"God, give the life of a galley unto he who wishes for one"

*Detail of the manoeuvre of
the mizzen yard of a lateen.*
(Muleta Mare Nostrum).

The galley undoubtedly lived longest out of all the military ships and, to a certain extent, had the worst reputation. That of a ship propelled "by blood", due to the strength of the oars, which is why slaves would be made to lend a hand and convicts forced to be galley slaves, one of the hardest and cruellest jobs that ever existed.

Regarding the galley and its galley slaves, there was little unanimity. The Mediterranean was the scene for many different cultures, some of them truly advanced socially, morally and intellectually. However, they were all linked by one common denominator, or perhaps, a similar black page in their histories. The Romans used slaves and prisoners, as did the Carthaginians. The Turks employed Christians or slaves – quite often it was the same - and the Christians likewise with their own Turkish slaves, convicts or those who had been enforced.

Such punishment was a constant in any country's civil law that had galleys, and it wasn't necessary to have committed any great crime, on occasion just robbing a simple loaf of bread was enough to condemn a man for two or three years.

There was one other option: that of selling oneself. Boarding for a specific length of time (a minimum of two years), voluntarily condemning

oneself to experience a life of hell. These galley slaves – known as *buena boga* - were quite often recruited in the most curious or least orthodox of ways. Among these it seems two were most common. The first combined necessity and gambling: a gambler who had lost was offered a loan to recover his position, one which would also rapidly disappear when playing with other gamblers who had the advantage. Once the money lender had spent all he had, he would claim the person he had lent the money to as his to offer as a galley slave as his failure to return the loan implied his amount paid on a galley. The second way was not only used repeatedly on galleys but also on many other ships, merchant or warships: the subject in question would have been intoxicated and on waking would find himself shackled to the bench, or at sea sailing on a voyage that would last many months or several years almost without ever touching port and subjected to a disciplinary code enforced via the "cat o'nine tails".

At a time when human life had only relative value, the fact that some hundreds of galley slaves, shackled to the benches, would sink with the ship or end up literally tearing off a foot in order to free themselves when the ship sank, did not shock anybody as in the end, the rabble – the name given to

The Majorcan catboat *Far de Formentera*. Restoration work. This boat was changed to mechanical propulsion and equipped with two diesel engines and two propellers.

these people and which even now is highly derogatory - were considered to be worth very little even though there were a few illustrious names among them. But in a certain way nobody was worth more than the price of their possible rescue.

The life of a galley slave was utterly wretched. And not only because of the physical effort involved; living conditions also had a great influence. Arriving on board he would be chained to his bench and only released to be thrown overboard – when he was dead - set free or, if the galley sergeant was sympathetic enough, to stop him going down with the sinking ship. The galley bench served the slave as bed and table, he lived crushed up against the other men and the floor beneath him was awash with all kinds of human waste.

The galleys of Lepanto took on board between 250 and 366 galley slaves, to which would be added another 200 who made up the crew and of these, 10-15 were commanders and specialists; 30-40 sailors; 8-10 artillery and 150 soldiers. The stench of the daily defecation of more than 300

men, as well as the inevitable vomit when the sea became a little choppy, and the sweat produced by so much toil, must have been intolerable after a few days at sea. It is said that the smell was so strong that a galley could be smelt before it came into view. Parasites multiplied in such conditions and numerous illnesses would decimate the galley slaves in a briny, damp, foul smelling atmosphere (in 1570 the Venetian fleet lost 40,000 men without having entered into battle, in the port of Zara) and also poisonous for the rest of the crew. But there was always one consolation for the suffering galley slave: nobody on board, not even those wearing a crown, be it purple or mitre, however much perfume they used, could consider themselves safe from the smell or the plague of numerous parasites unable to distinguish between noblemen and plebeians. So after just a few hours at sea our nobleman would be scratching and stinking as much as any other man on board.

The other extreme of the galley's history is that of the ships whose ornamentation and riches were

Detail of the bow of the Majorcan catboat 'Far de Formentera'.

Detail of the mizzen yard, sail and reef bands of the rigging on the Majorcan catboat 'Far de Formentera'.

beyond belief. These were the ships, especially those known as Captain and Royal ships, which dazzled with fine woods and metals, ivory and silk, paintings and tapestries. It is hardly surprising, then, that there were those eager to capture such a ship as if they succeeded they would become instantly wealthy and remain so for the rest of their days. The galley, in spite of being a ship with oars, did not often use these to travel unless the wind was unfavourable or the weather was set to change. Although in earlier times (Greek, Roman, etc.) galleys used square sails and a single mast, with the arrival of the lateen sail this type of sail was adopted with two masts both with mizzen yards and their corresponding lateen sails, which it seems were quite often two-coloured in vertical bands.

The jib was often smaller than the main (approximately 49-59 and 65-82 feet respectively), unlike the two-pieced (tack and *pena*) lateen yards, which, due to their great length, (82-98 feet) would often measure the same. The overall surface of the sails was no greater than 5,381 square feet, with sails of different sizes being used according to the strength of the wind.

The *Xabeck*, hound of the Mediterranean

The xabeck is one of the most authentic and best-known sailboats of the Mediterranean, with perhaps the most graceful appearance. Whether as a fishing boat, war or merchant ship, it achieved maximum fame through its constant use, as much by Berber pirates as by those who fought against them as it was fast and agile to manoeuvre, preferably using sails but also using oars if the occasion called for them.

The fine lines of its hull are famous, accentuating the great rake of its stem to which could also be added, or not, a long bowsprit. The poop deck stood out at the stern, projecting way beyond the sternpost, whose deck crossed the tiller of the rudder. The considerably arched deck forced the artillery, usually 12 to 18 cannons each side, to place themselves in the passage ways or corridors, in an arrangement very similar to that of certain fishing boats, which followed the shape of the deck stringer. In this way they were able to achieve a sufficiently high firing angle.

Although its displacement was not as a rule very great (that of the fishing xabecks would often be somewhere between 30 and 60 tons while the merchants and war xabecks between 300 and 400), there was one case which reached more than 600. In spite of being a boat that sailed exclusively in the Mediterranean, there was one which managed to cross the Atlantic.

Its rigging was very simple, three masts – the jib down at the bow and the mains and mizzen almost vertical on end – which supported both lateen sails, that of the jib with the bow handle anchored to the end of the bowsprit or the stem itself, meaning it could be accurately quartered in tacking. However, there were also cases of square, mystical xabecks.

In Spain, xabecks were first armed during the reign of Carlos II at the end of the seventeenth century, and remained in service until 1827 when the last one was withdrawn. The most famous figure

The Majorcan catboat Far de Formentera, sailing 'a la buena' that is, with the mast windward, in which the sail forms one single pocket.

on board the xabecks was undoubtedly the Majorcan Antonio "Toni" Barceló, who from his humble and modest position as skipper, climbed up the ranks to become lieutenant general of the Spanish Navy, playing a part on several of its ships.

The versatile felucca

The felucca was another typically Mediterranean ship. With a long and light hull, it was related to the xabeck family and also used in numerous activities, although the most usual were for fishing and cabotage, although it also excelled as a coastguard and customs launch.

Its displacement was usually no more than 100 tons and was equipped with a rigging that in its best-known version (a main down at the bow, a small mizzen and a long boom, with both lateen and a flying jib, with a total maximum surface of about 1,076 square feet) eventually became a classic. Despite it being associated with North African

countries due to its birthplace (Algeria, Libya and Tunisia) and also used in the slave trade, in its most glorious times it was related more to the countries and coasts of the Iberian-Italo-French spectrum and trade, receiving very specific names in accordance with the geographical area in question ("barca de mitjana" in Catalonia; "felucca" in Italy, etc.).

For a good part of the last two centuries its activity of cabotage was tireless, being the only link for many populations – from the south of France to Cape of Gata, in Almería – with the important ports between those keeping it active and in constant trade. Its activity along the east coast of Spain started to decrease from the mid-nineteenth century onwards, when the arrival of the railway cut the cost of transport and also made it easier.

The external appearance of the different types, according to its job, presented various characteristics. The stern was one of the details that most differentiated the area or origin of construction as

The Majorcan catboat Far de Formentera, on its arrival in the bay of Cadaqués (Girona), to take part in the 1993 lateen sail boats reunion (VI Trobada de barques de vela llatina).

Side view of the Majorcan catboat, with 'mitjana', Alzina rigging. Note that the main, apart from sailing 'a la mala', carries reef bands.

well as the age of the boat; it varied from square with stern davits to that of transom, with counter, of two sections or round, and also varied according to its particular activity. So, those used for cabotage, would often have the poop deck projecting at the counter, the spar sticking out of its upper part to which was secured the clew cringle of the mizzen. In contrast, feluccas used for fishing had a sternpost that curved outwards leaning towards the bow, with the rudder following the shape. The measurements could range between 39 and 59 feet in length and 9 and 15 in breadth, with a small freeboard. The crew would be no more than 30 men.

Other ships with a lateen sail

The Mystic

The Mystic was a cargo ship, although there were some that were armed and used by pirates, with two or three masts rigged with lateen sails and a bowsprit with flying jib, widely used along the Catalan and Tunisian coasts. Like so many other types of ships its rigging evolved considerably, to a point where one was totally square and another composite in which fore-and-aft sails were mixed with lateen and square.

The Pink ('pinc' in Catalan)

Originally the pink was a ship with lateen rigging very similar to the xabeck, but it differed in its top sides being higher, its bow fuller and draught greater. According to several historians, the pink's main frame was more at the bow than in other ships and had more beam on waterline. One characteristic that was particularly unusual, although by no means rare, was the fact that some pinks had their mizzen mast displaced towards the port to allow for the manoeuvre of the rudder arm.

There were also Genovese and French pinks, some with truly curious rigging (there are records of a Genovese pink with complete square rigging

Detail of the boulter boat Capitán Argüello. Reef bands and rigging work.

The "Santa Espina". The great strength that a lateen sail exercises over its yard is noticeable. *Right,* group of boats with lateen sails lying to at the start of the competition. First is the *Capitán Argüello,* with all its rigging hoisted.

The hull and sail together, while being a whole, can vary immensely. Compare the hull and rigging of this boat with the others. *Right,* catboat sailing *'a la mala'* or *'contra el árbol'* in the middle of Cadaqués bay (Girona), a town considered one of the Costa Brava's most typical and beautiful.

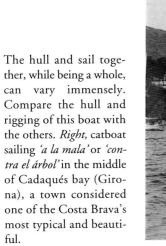

in two of its three masts and two extremely long mizzen yards above deck). The most common rigging was very similar to that of the xabeck, although there were also some with one or two crossed masts. Despite being a ship mainly used in cabotage, the odd one did reach the ports of the Bay of Biscay and it was not unknown for them to travel as far as the West Indies. Although their usual displacement was no more than 100 tons, there were some that were greater such as the *San Francisco de Paula*, which was more than 200, making it the second ship to transport directly from Barcelona to Veracruz, in 1747, before the free trade decree with America was announced. It remained in this role until the mid-nineteenth century.

The Ketch ('quetx' in Catalan)

The ketch is said to have been a boat whose rigging evolved backwards, or rather, that it started off with square rigging which was replaced by fore-and-aft and lateen rigging. It must be pointed out that the Mediterranean ketch has very little, or nothing, in common with other types of rigging also known as ketch. A present day ketch – two masts with spanker sail and topsail or bermudian or Marconi rigging – and another from the seventeenth century, from the United States and England, with two masts with square rigging, spanker sail and flying jibs.

The Mediterranean ketch was not very attractive where its hull – schooner or pilot boat – was concerned. Its rigging, however, was quite the opposite. Several naval historians claim its original rigging was mainly square (in the eighteenth century and beginning of the nineteenth it was equipped with a main, main topmast, and in the mizzen a topgallant and lateen). However, at the beginning of the nineteenth century, its rigging was altered to that of a slightly lowered foresail with a lateen and flying jib, next to a main with spanker sail and topsail. There is sufficient documentation of its construction with this rigging in the shipyards of Lloret de Mar, near Girona, in the second half of the nineteenth century.

The Saetia ('sagetia' in Catalan)

Very little is known about the Saetia, at least the type used for high seas sailing in the latter half

of the eighteenth century. In a doctoral thesis concerning the Catalan merchant navy of that time, it states that there were many Saetia in the ocean going merchant fleet, whose more classical rigging consisted of three masts (the foresail very low down at the bow, with main and mizzen on end) and a bowsprit. It carried both lateen sails, serving the bowsprit to secure the end of the foresail tack, but had no flying jib.

Ocean sailing led to a necessary change of rigging from lateen to square, starting with the foresail. It permanently disappeared at the end of the eighteenth century, being replaced by frigates and brigs.

The Tartan

Documented from the eighteenth century, the Tartan was used a lot in the Mediterranean for coastal trade and fishing, particularly along the Franco-Catalan coast. Its capacity was small – between 20 and 90 tons – and its rigging usually made up of one mast perpendicular to and halfway along the keel, that hoisted a lateen sail and flying topsail. A boom was fitted with a flying jib and occasionally a little mizzen at the stern also carried another small lateen.

The Velachero ('Llondro' in Catalan)

With one of the most characteristic riggings of the Mediterranean, the velachero disappeared at the end of the nineteenth century. Its hull was very similar to that of the pink, although its displacement smaller, as a rule around 50 tons, although in others it was 80 and with the *Virgen del Carmen*, 105. Its rigging was very striking and joined the crossed yards with the lateen mizzen yards; the most habitual consisted of a crossed foresail (polacre, with only two pieces) with three sails (foresail, fore-topsail and topgallant) and flying jibs (no more than two or three), a main with lateen and a small mast rope at the stern.

Fishing boats

Sail fishing is something that became part of history in its own right. First was the arrival of the internal combustion engine, at first horrific motors whose deafening roar shook the beaches, followed by faster and quieter models which star-

The personality of the Obock is very clear in this view from bow starboard.

In this view of the *Obock* from fashion piece starboard one can imagine it comes from somewhat exotic descent.

ted to throw the classic fisherman out of his thousand-year-old trade. Later new, more productive ways of fishing that also relied on mechanical propulsion, continued to relegate the traditional fisherman, unable to come to terms with so much innovation, to the beach. In the end it was the pressing need to adopt profit-making business criteria that put an end to what had been an art but was now nothing more than simple business.

So, in just a couple of generations, helped by an industrialised, frenetic tourist industry that converted what had once been beautiful fishing villages into huge hotel complexes, the friendly, well-loved figure of the fisherman with leathery tanned skin, sitting on his chair beside his cottage or sitting on the ground repairing nets, has disappeared from our coasts only to be found in museums.

Meanwhile, the fishing boats, named by the experts according to their construction, art or use (seiners, catboats, boulters, sardine boats, trammel nets, etc.) have permanently disappeared from the French and Spanish Mediterranean co-

asts. Little trace is left of them other than a few examples, survivors of innumerable runs, preserved through constant sacrifice on behalf of a few unflagging enthusiasts, often criticised and labelled as eccentrics. They are like relics from the past, which have been saved from downfall or widespread barbarity.

The Bou (Ox)

In ancient times "bou" (ox) was the name given to the art of trawler fishing in the Mediterranean. The name of this art could well have come from the position and way the boats sailed in pairs, slightly apart in order to keep the mouth of the net open. This recalled the yoke carried by a couple of oxen, although linguists disagree and believe that it came from the Latin "bolus", meaning the act of throwing nets.

Therefore, boats that fished in this way were called "bous" and were usually all very alike, with the same rigging so that the trawling itself was uniform. The typical rigging of "ox boats" was lateen, with just one mast and bowsprit or boom, with a lateen sail and flying jib.

The hull was similar to that of the other types of fishing boats, although with slight variations or peculiarities and like the catboat, was very common in the Mediterranean.

The catboat

Even though there is information showing that the catboat was a type of boat with a long and narrow hull, similar to the felucca, but with much less rigging, consisting of just one lateen sail, other documents contradict this, stating it could also have used a flying jib and a small mizzen sail, making it comparable with the felucca.

Nevertheless, it is more commonly believed that the catboat was a small boat, mainly dedicated to fishing or small scale cabotage. Its rigging was made up of only one mast and one single lateen sail.

As for the hull, a number of variations and features associated with the area or village it was built can be found. The most typical were constructions with a lot of camber and lateral galleries, fixed gunwales or ones that could be detached by a system of vertically-sliding boards on guides. A large part of the deck is taken up by a hatchway to

which access is gained through several flaps or quarters. In one of these the mast is accommodated through a cut or a part that has been sawn down. As they are boats that use oars or sails indiscriminately for propulsion they are fitted with rowlocks, positioned at the appropriate points.

Depending on whether the hulls were for careening close to the shore or anchoring in shelter, they were fitted with the appropriate chainplates or not, so that they would stay righted and being able to slide over the runners.

One catboat that has survived is the *Far de Formentera*, built in Majorca in the 1920s and linked to the Ministry of Public Works' lighthouse service for many years. Its work for the Ministry ceased, and little interest was shown in it until later in the 1990s when it was recovered

The lateen sail is also suitable for small craft. Note how this boat's mast leans more towards the bow and the yard is also hoisted from a point nearer the bow.

In this small boat the system of binding the tack grip to the yard to the stem itself seems perfect.

thanks to the efforts of an organisation known as "Barcelona, fes-te a la mar" (Barcelona, open up to the sea) under the auspices of Barcelona Council. It was radically reconstructed and its original appearance was restored, rigged with lateen sail and flying jib.

The Muleta

The muleta was a small fishing boat that was used in methods known as 'l'art' or 'a la saltada' in Catalan, using either the lateen sail or oars and due to its shallow draught was suitable for mixed use, either coastal or river.

Typical of the Delta del Ebro area, it was also used as a regatta launch in villages' patron saint's day festivities. Particularly famous were those celebrated in L'Ampolla in Tarragona at San Juan in June when the boats would carry a crew of six oarsmen and one helmsman.

In 1990 one of these boats was recovered in a very poor state, built in 1956 in Tortosa near Tarragona by the shipbuilders Hermanos Vilas (Vilas Brothers). It was transferred to the workshop school 'El Far' (The Lighthouse) which the organisation "Barcelona, fes-te a la mar" established in Barceloneta, where it was reconstruc-

ted. Today it is a valuable piece and one of the scarce valuable pieces of Spain's maritime heritage.

The Sardinier

The sardiniers (boats mainly but not exclusively used for sardine fishing) were wider than catboats and proportionately had less upper works. Their completely flat bottom made them particularly suitable for careening close to the shore. They were dragged up onto the beach on special capstans, helped by three skates that made up the keel itself and two small lateral keels or chainplates. The stem was straight – later on it became more slanting and the sternpost slightly curved - which meant the rudder had to follow the same shape. The great central hatchway was defined by *guardamares*, boards that were placed on their sides that also acted as a support or coaming in the quarters of the hatchway. Its length would usually be between 19 and 26 feet, with a displacement of up to 2 tons.

One characteristic of the different ways of fishing using lights to attract the fish is that of the small boats that carry the lights. Today, as fishing fleets do not careen close to the shore, it is something that has completely disappeared and is now almost unheard of. In the past, although they could still be seen right up to the 1960s, it was a very colourful and attractive sight to see the vast array of boats of all sizes and colours close to Mediterranean Spanish beaches, along with small boats in which the great, shining petrol steam lights seemed even brighter and visible in comparison.

And if the boats alone were attractive, their presence adding to a landscape that in itself was already captivating, one can imagine how picturesque it must have looked with the addition of onlookers who would go there every evening at sunset, when the fleets arrived and helped with the careening.

Manoeuvres with lateen sails

It is not the aim of this book to describe the manoeuvre of a lateen sail in detail. However, a few special features often attract considerable attention from being totally visible during sailing, and are therefore worthy of a mention.

One of the most typical features of the lateen sail is the hoisted yard. Block and tackles low, high and yard halyard.

We have already seen that the lateen sail is a type of rigging particularly suitable for sailing bowline or with cross winds and not really so for downwind sailing.

The reason for this is that being lateen rigging supported by a mizzen yard that has two fixed points, one in the mast itself and the other in the stem, it cannot open up or cross the wind as easily as the spanker sails or Marconis. Nevertheless, that does not mean that with lateen sails one cannot sail downwind, as downwind is precisely one of the positions in which this type of sails have a most curious appearance.

There are two ways in which a lateen can be positioned to work with the wind at the stern. The mizzen yard can either be high and crossed, known in sailing as 'cross', *a la bobera* or 'luff-sailing', or it can be secured by the point of the tack to the side – to sail "mule-eared, donkey-eared, hare-eared or cat-whiskered" – in which the position of the sail and mizzen yard are reminiscent of a donkey or mule's ear.

In the first case the ends of the extreme of the tack ('orsaprop' and 'devant') are secured very long in the bow and stern, with which the mizzen yard is raised thanks to the sheet passing through a loop over the deck. The mizzen yard adopts a position similar to that of a yard of cross or square rigging, while the sail stays in a triangular position, with the mizzen yard above and the sheet tack below. Ideally the sail should work 'a la buena' - that is, with the mast windward, in which the sail forms one single pocket - but it can also be used with the mast against the wind – 'a la mala'.

In the second case, typical on boats with two masts, whether it is sailing 'a la buena' or 'a la mala', even though the former may be more effective, the sail pockets fully as it stays wide open on the side thanks to the secured end of the tack slowing down until it is in front of the mast. This way of crossing the mizzen yard was changed to each hand on boats with two sails, therefore the figure that was seen from afar at the bow was certainly that of the 'donkey's ears'.

Another small boat with lateen sail and jib, seen from the side. Note the respective positions of the mast and yard.

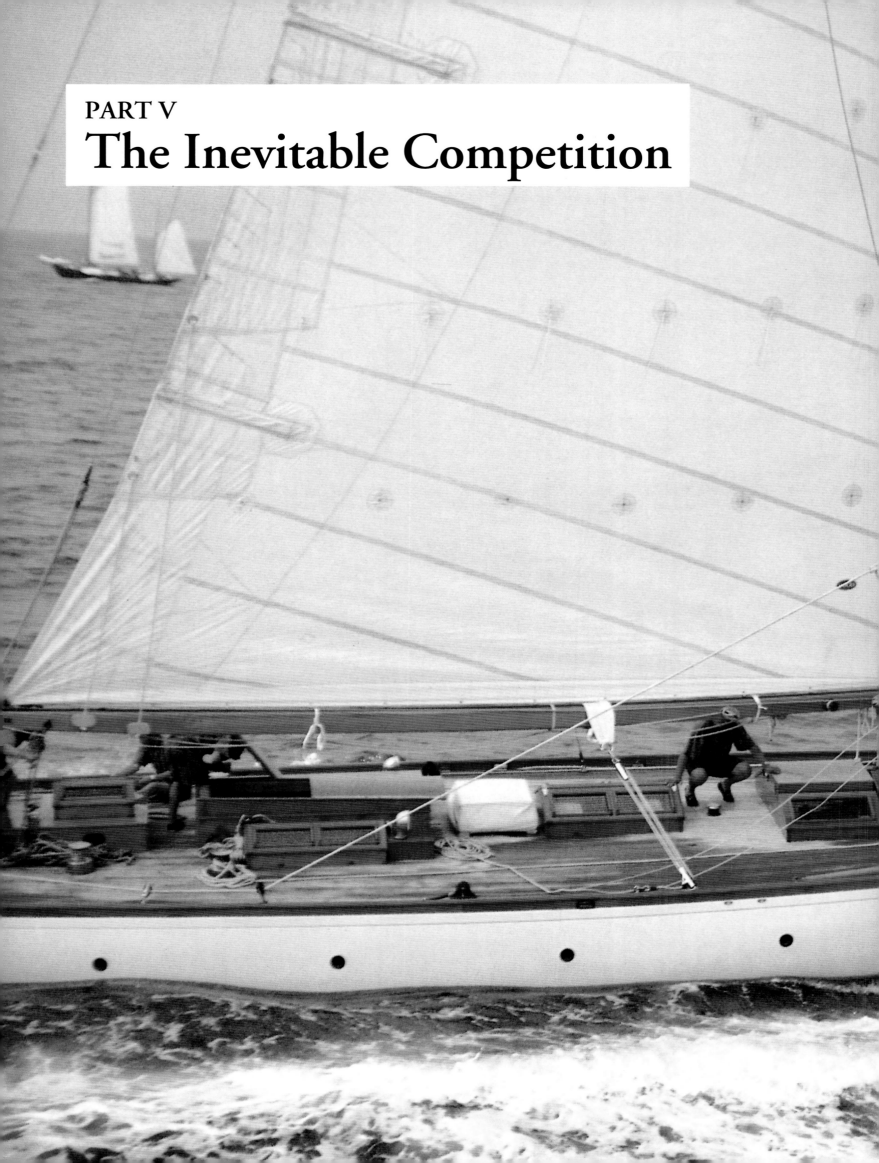

PART V
The Inevitable Competition

Before taking a look at the evolution of maritime competition there is a language point to be considered. There are a few differences of concept between the words race and regatta. As a general rule a regatta is considered a competition played out between two or more boats, while a race is similar in meaning but applied to on land vehicles. Race can also be applied to the regular line of sailing and, a lot of the time, by simple extension or chronic ignorance of marine vocabulary, is the name given to a competition between motor boats, even though motor boating pilots prefer to use the word regatta to race.

Competition is something inherent in human beings, and almost as old. With the modern Olympic Games one is reminded of the games that took place in ancient Greece, during which all other activity stopped that was not truly Olympic, including war. It was considered indisputable that there had to be some form of regatta between ships. What is unknown is whether the competition was between people of the same nationality, or perhaps between Greeks and Persians, in peace times.

In Rome itself all kinds of games were celebrated, from chariot races to gladiator fights, although it could be said that the leitmotiv had degenerated slightly as the idea was not so much to win a crown of laurels or prove who was the strongest, but just to come out alive.

From the regatta for reasons of pure necessity...

In a more maritime aspect it is very likely – at least it would seem logical as there were boats that were more or less suitable – that in a world in which such types of games were held, they must also have lavished on regattas. In this sense who can resist imagining one tribune defiantly challenging another with cries of "my galley slaves are stronger and can stand up to more than yours" It is also possible that the bet in question was in no

way amusing for its main protagonists: the galley slaves, who undoubtedly, must have been exhausted after a regatta which, at best, and if they won, would require superhuman effort or, at worst, and if they lost, besides the great effort there would also be rather unpleasant consequences.

Whatever the case may have been, it seems that the first historically documented regatta is described in Virgil's Aenid. It was held near present day Trapani, in Sicily in which four triremes took part, poor galley slaves! The story tells of bets that resulted in many lives or great amounts of money being lost, a curious fact since on many occasions the challenge had started off as something trivial and had not seemed that it would go on to be taken so seriously.

It is not known, or at least we cannot be sure, whether there were sailing regattas in the dark times of the Middle Ages. If they did exist, they must also have had their own particular form of peremptory salvation because, if we think about the attacks of Viking ships on other vessels, and

the usual terrible fate reserved for the passengers and crews of the attacked ships, it seems doubtless that there were regattas or something similar. They would certainly have been hard-fought and disputed but for no other more serious reason – although this would seem important enough – than to escape from the rage of those "barbarians of the north" whose brutality was such that it led to the prayer "De furore normanorum; libera nos Dómine" ('Free us, o Lord, from the fury of the Norsemen') being included in the litanies.

Entering the period from the end of the fifteenth century and the discovery of America, whose great riches led to the reappearance of piracy, something already familiar in ancient Greece, sailing regattas were reintroduced with no greater aim than escape and saving lives and property. In this respect it is worth mentioning the existence of pirates whose misdeeds were truly predatory, so much so that any boat would make sure there was the maximum distance between itself and a pirate ship, without the need for any further justification.

The start of a regatta of classic boats of all types, in particular competition sailing boats.

Top competition boats are real gems that have to be carefully looked after and tuned as if they were violins.

After every regatta the manoeuvres are left perfectly clear and ready.

Later on, more civilised times with greater moral values saw a very different type of regatta appear. Here the competition was carried out partly through a pure spirit of survival and partly through a self-justified commercial necessity. This was the slave or "ebony trade" as it was known euphemistically, along with the smuggling of goods, whether war contraband or just plain smuggling.

Slave ships were usually very fast. Speed had become a necessity in order to both maintain the cargo quality and freshness, and to be faster than the ships that pursued them. The first, in the eyes of those who dealt in this trade, was a pure and simple commercial necessity. The shorter the journey, the shorter the time with an overcrowded load; and less time of overcrowding meant better appearance, less chance of illness and an easier or more profitable sale. The second was really a consequence of the first as any slave trader caught red-handed would lose his load and its corresponding value. It was also likely that he would be hanged from a yard without trial. And although today this type of trade is considered totally abhorrent, it must be remembered that it was still the most important and profitable trade in the seventeenth, eighteenth and a good part of

the nineteenth century and at that time few found it distasteful and little thought was given to the many great fortunes that had been made from this activity, money that was later purified – known today as 'laundered' - in small percentages with financing from various social and even pious works. Many of these fortunes have survived to the present day without anybody questioning their origins.

As far as those involved in pure and simple smuggling were concerned, their needs were not that different from today. It is already known that present day smugglers' boats often develop their activity in two ways, at great speed or by trying to pass unnoticed. The first is really a regatta between smugglers and police forces (it is said that modern "off-shore" motorboat competitions were born from the daring feats of the North American smugglers in the time of Prohibition) and at that time this type of regatta also took place because of a strong desire to escape the duly imposed punishments and sentences that were much harder than today.

...to that of more commercial purposes

Earlier we saw that the word 'race' also has a

114

maritime meaning. There have been many maritime races, some of them quite remarkable and in which the most glorious pages of sailing history have been written. Some of the most famous races were the tea and wool races, from Australia and California; wheat races and nitrate from Chile. For the Spanish the most memorable were those from America, the Philippines, Lima, Havana, the West Indies, those of coal or dried beef.

All of them had in common transporting goods or passengers on a regular line, having established real competitions between the different boats, as arriving before or after one's rival could have a direct effect on the business transacted, such as a greater quantity of voyages, passengers or a better price obtained for the goods delivered.

There were fleets and ships that won fame and prestige in some of the races mentioned. And figures such as the Finnish Eriksson who won renown in the Australian wheat race that continued until 1939. Or F. L. Laeisz from Hamburg in the Chilean nitrate race. However, the names that shone most brightly were always those of the ships themselves. Particularly outstanding were the following: *Ariel, Cutty Sark, Lacing, Pamir, Passat, Potosi, Preussen, Teaping, Serica, Thermopilae, Sir Lancelot* and many others.

The tea race

It is well known that tea, the English national drink, is not produced in England but instead imported from Asia. For a good part of the nineteenth century, the transport from China to the British metropolis was carried out on board rapid clippers that, departing habitually from Foochow would set off on a long crossing around Cape Horn, often lasting 3 to 5 months, depending on the winds, and the ship that arrived first in London would win a special prize of 100 guineas.

With this in mind the captains would sail their ships furiously hoping to get there first and pick

When there is a break competitors do not exist; all boats are moored together in happy camaraderie.

Two very different boats competing in the same regatta; a schooner with stays and a Marconi ketch.

up the prize. Besides the honour of having won, the sum was enough to bedazzle anyone, and it didn't even have to be shared out among the crew or with the ship owner.

On 30th May, 1886, the by now famous clippers *Ariel, Fiery Cross, Serica* and *Teaping* set sail from Foochow, at intervals of no more than a few hours. For a good part of the crossing the *Fiery Cross* was ahead of the rest, with the *Ariel* and the *Teaping* following close behind and the *Serica* a little further back. On passing the island of Santa Elena the *Teaping* overtook the *Fiery Cross, Serica* and *Ariel*, in that order. At the is-

lands of Cape Verde the *Ariel* was in the lead, reaching the English Channel still ahead of the rest. However, the *Teaping* was in sight and the two ships sailed up the Thames together, both docking in London on the afternoon of 7th September, in front of a crowd that had been fervently following the contest. The two ships were both considered the winners and the prize was shared between them.

Another contest that looked on the cards was between the *Thermopilae* and the *Cutty Sark*. In 1872 both ships left Shanghai on the same day, each carrying a load of tea (the *Thermopilae*

1,196,460 pounds and the *Cutty Sark* 1,303,000 pounds) and it was anticipated that there would be something like a repeat of the famous regatta six years earlier, as the *Cutty Sark* was in the lead at the beginning. Only 28 days later, on passing the Sunda Strait, the *Thermopilae* was ahead by one mile and a half, but fresh winds entered the fray, allowing the *Cutty Sark* to take a 400-mile lead. Unfortunately, the *Cutty Sark* got caught in a gale and lost its rudder, but despite having carried a makeshift one, it arrived in London a week after the *Thermopilae*, which had completed the voyage in just 115 days.

The wool race

The wool race was not as exciting as the tea race – especially as there were no money prizes to be won – neither did it take place in similar times. In the years of the wool race steam was winning the battle outright against sailing ships and both ship owners and passengers alike preferred using steam ships because of their better punctuality and greater comfort for everyone. This meant that the famous sailing ships of the then recent past were relegated to less famous and lesser known crossings.

The ships that took part in the wool race from distant Australia to the European ports or textile centres would often make the outward voyage loaded with general cargo and coal. On the return voyage they would be carrying variable amounts of wool in balls, normally numbering between 3,000 and 6,000, depending on the ship. Both the *Cutty Sark* and the *Thermopilae* took part in that race, their voyages lasting between seventy and a hundred days.

There were many other ships that also participated in that long, tiring crossing, a great many ended up being scrapped without ever receiving any fame or recognition. One such example was the *Torrens,* a ship that carried both cargo and passengers and was in service from 1875 until 1903 when it was sold to an Italian shipping company, finally being scrapped in 1910. In 1880-1881 it completed the fastest voyage between Plymouth and Adelaide in just 65 days. Another similar case was the *Salamis,* a ship of 1,130 tons record gross, owned by G. Thompson & Co. It sailed between Melbourne and London on a regular basis. It was sold in 1899 to some Norwegian ship owners who used it in guano or nitrate races. In 1905 it was wrecked in the South Pacific near the island of Maldon.

The Chile nitrate races and the Australia grain races

Another of the races that enjoyed its heyday for several years was that of nitrate from Chile.

Modern intensive farming demands a nitrogenous fertiliser and before good quality, reasonably priced artificial fertilisers became available, the only one of this type was the natural kind. Chile possessed great sodium nitrate deposits

117

All the details, sails, mano-euvres, ironwork, decks, show just how much love and care has been invested in the boat.

BLANC BLEU

During free time is when maintenance tasks are carried out.

which it distributed to Europe and other countries by means of great fleets of sailing ships.

In this respect the great sailing ship – which evolved from the wooden hull to that of iron, and later to steel, also with metal rigging - that had gone from displacements of less than 1,000 tons to 5,000 in ships such as the *Preussen* in only 60 years, proved to be a very suitable vessel as its freightage was cheaper than that of steam. At the end of last century, such ships started to be used for this task, many of which already veterans of similar battles but had been recovered when the races no longer held any interest or had just disappeared altogether.

Two of the shipping companies that were most involved in the nitrate races were the German R. F. Laeisz – the famous "P Line" – and the French A. D. Bordes. The second went as far as including 36 large ships for the purpose; the first offered the attraction of being the most beautiful, fastest sailing ships of the time, certainly the greatest that had ever been built. Even when it started with the frigate *Polynesia*, shortly afterwards the new four-masted barracks *Pangani* and *Pamir* were introduced, along with the giants with five masts *Potosi* (with barrack rigging) and the *Preussen,* the only five masted frigate ever built in sailing history.

The ships of the Laeisz were seized by the powerful winners after the First World War, although some were recovered after 1920 when the German nitrate fleet returned to sail.

Out of all of these, the one which best survived was the *Pamir,* which, acquired in 1931 by the Finnish Gustav Erikson, was consecrated to the wheat race between Australia and Europe until 1939. After the Second World War it was bought by a New Zealand shipping company who used it to cover its route between Wellington and San Francisco. At the beginning of the 1950s it was rented out as a training ship for the German merchant navy, being lost in a violent storm in the Atlantic in 1957, with a great loss of human lives.

The aforementioned Finnish captain Gustav Erikson acquired, between 1913 and 1939, a sizeable fleet of sailing ships of all types based in Mariehamn, a port in the Aland Islands, near the Finnish coast, mainly used in the Australian wheat race. The most outstanding of this fleet were the *Passat, Lawbill, Archibald, Russell, Herzogin Cecilie, Olivebank, Pommern, Penang, Viking, L'Avenir, Hougomont, Mosbulu* and the aforementioned *Pamir.* For many years these ships transported their cargo of wheat from the ports of the southern coast of Australia to Great Britain, making, as a rule, the outward journey with a ballast cargo, although occasionally they also transported wood from Finland itself to the ports of South Africa.

It is very likely that besides the *Pamir*, the best-known ship of Laiesz's fleet was the *Herzogin Cecilie,* a four masted frigate, that won the wheat regatta eight times before it was wrecked in 1936. It took an average of 100 days to sail from Australia to Europe.

All these majestic boats, evicted by the machine, progress, speed and competition, finally disappeared from the oceans' surface. The number of survivors can be counted on one hand, now exhibits in museums and similar institutions. Today, ocean navigation in large sailing ships has been reduced to training schools.

Sports regattas

Records documenting the existence of sailing as pleasure date back to the beginning of the seventeenth century, in which paintings can be seen of regattas between Dutch yachts. The word 'yacht', which originates from the Dutch word 'jaghtschip' (pursuer boat) is used for boats solely destined to pleasure sailing, but it is also used to define a type of small boat with just one mast fitted or not with a topsail and main that could be anything from a primitive spanker sail to a *tarquina*[1]. The rest of the rigging is made up of a couple of flying jibs attached to the bowsprit. The hull is notable for its flamboyant and over elaborate ornamentation and lateral keels.

This type of rigging and boat, first apparent in the seventeenth century, continued to evolve until it became one that was very variable, although generally it carried a couple of masts with lateen sails, a yard and flying jibs. More recently, as the yacht has become more identified with competition and faster boats have appeared, one can see very differing forms of rigging, the majority of them with a spanker sail base, topsail, staysails and flying jibs. It would also seem that the Venetians and Genovese owned pleasure boats, except that they used the traditional Mediterranean sail, the lateen.

We also know of the existence of certain royal ships from much earlier times, such as the royal ship belonging to Cleopatra that could only ever be used for pleasure, given that, according to Plutarch, its sails were made of pure silk, the stern of gold and the oars silver plated. Neither should the possibility be rejected that Chinese and Arab civilisations also owned similar ships, a theory supported and defended by famous naval historians. Especially when one considers that these peoples particularly distinguished themselves by placing particular importance on pleasure, opulence and refinement.

In 1650, Charles II was proclaimed king of England, only to be defeated the following year by Oliver Cromwell. Having fled to France and Holland he became familiar with the 'jagchts' owned by the Dutch nobility. His enthusiasm for them was such that the burger master of Amsterdam presented him with one, which was to follow the king when he returned to England in 1660. In 1661 there was also another yacht in England, the king's brother the Duke of York's, taking part in the first ever regatta recorded in written documents. The boats taking part were the *Jenny* (the king's boat) and the *Anne* (belonging to the Duke of York). The bet was one hundred pounds which the *Jenny* won.

The rest is easy to imagine, with this new opportunity before them, the English nobility also took to the activity of pleasure sailing and started to make bets with each other. From here to the birth of 'yachting' there was just one step. A step that was taken between the years of 1660 and 1670 when no less than 26 yachts were built, all of which were owned by royalty and nobility. Hence 'the sport of kings' was born.

Not long after, in 1720, the Royal Yacht Club, the first yachting club in history, was founded. It was within the inlet of Cork, a sheltered cove in the south of Ireland, on one of its islands. In 1775, it became what at the time was known as the Cumberland Fleet and is now called the Royal Thames Yacht Club. The first Spanish clubs appeared a little more than a century later, and included the Club Náutico de Tarragona (Tarragona Yacht Club) (1878), Real Club Mediterráneo de Málaga (1879) and Real Club de Regatas (1881), what is now the Real Club Marítimo de Barcelona.

America's Cup

That the America's Cup is the most famous sailing competition in the world seems absolutely

indisputable. Equally undeniable is that in Spain it has always been treated as practically an unknown event, not down to a lack of interest on Spain's part but a doubly unfortunate reason: Spain had never taken part in this type of challenge and the media had never felt much inclination towards nautical matters. Even today, if there is any news coverage concerning boats and the sea, it almost always contains strong criticism or is very dismissive, if not downright pejorative.

The America's Cup started off somewhat insignificantly but has become the most important sailing regatta in the world. Many of the most important technological advances have been achieved in many different fields thanks to this contest. Large amounts of money and effort have been offered on behalf of the participating countries. The day that Australia won the Cup, although they lost it shortly after, was celebrated almost as much as the end of the Second World War, being considered a glory and national achie-

vement. But Australia is an island-continent and Spain just a peninsula that is almost an island.

On 17th July, 1845, the New York Yacht club celebrated what was considered the first regatta in the United States. Nine yachts took part and the amount obtained from signing up fees was awarded to the winner to buy themselves a commemorative cup.

The following year, the same club organised another regatta won by the sloop *María,* which came out as the fastest of its time. In 1847, when American sponsors and enthusiasts came to hear of the presence of the English *Pearl,* they decided to set a challenge which was taken up by the yacht *Coquette,* a boat with similar characteristics. The North American boat won by 55 seconds.

In 1850 the English invited their rivals from the New York club to participate in a regatta that was to take place the following year in Cowes, to mark the occasion of the great Universal Exhibition of Industry. The Americans, still exul-

A challenge is when two boats sail one against the other. They can be any kind of boat as long as they have accepted the challenge.

121

Since then, the challenge has been held 28 times, and each time won by America. But in 1983, the American boat *Liberty*, at the command of the sponsor Dennis Conner, was defeated by the *Australia II*. The so coveted America's Cup had changed hands for the second time in its history. To say that in Australia the victory was celebrated would give a pale idea of what happened. The occasion was considered something of a national victory – just as in the United States, but the other way round – with the crew becoming famous celebrities.

The Americans did not, however, give up. They designed a new boat that involved the most advanced space and computer technology. The defeat by Australia struck the American competitors hard, almost considering it a concern of national honour. The result of such commotion was only to be expected, the *Stars and Stripes* (a blatant reference to the national flag) beat the Australian *Kookaburra III* in the following challenge in 1987. In technology, as in yachting, the North Americans could rest easy, they were back at the top.

But today's boats, despite being extraordinarily fast and born of latest technology, have neither the charm nor the lineage of their ancestors, the true 'lords of the sea', or gentleman's racing yachts,

tant from their recent victory with the *Coquette*, immediately accepted the invitation forming a syndicate of six members that took on the construction costs of the schooner *America*, designed by the young engineer Steer. On arriving in Cowes it soon became evident that it was an extraordinarily fast boat with great manoeuvrability. At 9.55 in the morning on 22nd August, following the usual cannon shot, the regatta commenced (at that time it was normal to set off at anchor). Seven miles into the race, the *America* was in fifth place when the wind got up. The combination of a fresh wind and the sea in its favour helped the *America* overtake its opponents and leave the boat on its tail, the cutter *Aurora*, a staggering twelve miles behind. But due to the tide and the wind dying down the *America* lost its considerable lead which was reduced to just a mile on reaching the race's finish.

That modest cup, which for several years was held by Commodore John C. Stevens, life and soul of the owner syndicate of the boat, was passed on to the display cabinets of the New York Yacht Club in 1857, where it stayed as a prize for a challenge regatta, but with the provision that the future winner keep it in equal condition.

122

which have sadly all but disappeared.

It is inevitable that in such an important and historical competition, apart from being hallowed with patriotic colours and national honour, there should be a considerable number of anecdotes. It is very probable that if half of those that are told were true there would have to have been twice the number of challenges that have been held. To relate them all would detract from the meaning of this work, besides being a nigh impossible feat. However, we can't resist mentioning two which, if not the best are certainly our favourites.

It is said that in the first regatta, Queen Victoria was following the contest from her royal yacht *Victoria and Albert*. At one point in the regatta, when the *America* was 12 miles ahead of the English competitor, the Queen asked one of her companions (some say it was the prime minister) "Who is in second place?" to which she received the laconic, succinct and suggestive reply "There is no second, your Majesty". Another that remains in the collection of anecdotes is that whenever any of the small group of people from the New York

Yacht Club, almost perpetual owner of the trophy, were showing the cup to some guest, they would always say that the day the trophy was lost, the head of the person to lose it would be substituted in the display cabinet. Fortunately this never happened, but it is said that the loser was considered little less than a pariah while the cup was in the hands of the Australians. On winning back the cup this treatment was diluted slightly, but not totally as it did not return to the hands of the New York Yacht Club but to their most direct rivals, the San Diego Yacht Club.

Classic Ship Regattas

It is hard to know exactly why somebody, clearly a great sea and boat enthusiast, started to feel a certain frustration or shame regarding the sending of excellent ships to be burnt on the fire, ships which could still offer hours of healthy enjoyment. It is also clear that whoever thought this did not do so under the usual criteria of cost and

All sail together towards the buoy. Fewer boats are often found upon arrival as the boats become distanced out from one another.

profitability, but with their thoughts concentrating on other more subtle and impalpable values, undoubtedly of greater consideration and merit than the others. The sailing and maintenance of a classic ship requires being a navigator, antiquarian, naval architect, ship carpenter and lover of the sea and boats all rolled into one.

A classic ship is made entirely from wood in as much as its rigging, hull, ribs and deck, while cotton sails and rope are obviously made from natural fibres; its fittings are classic made of that type of bronze that needs to be polished while the deck has to be scrubbed and washed down as it was in the glorious days of sailing in which the work was constant. The owners of such a ship know that the word fibreglass is totally banned just as are synthetic textiles and stainless steel. Their ships are not only their means of sailing, they are also an essential, indispensable component of sailing itself, and they creak, moan and breathe in an attempt to affirm their own personality. They are almost living beings with a heart and soul and as such need to be understood and loved.

Classic ship regattas are not regattas in the true sense of the word. They are regattas in one respect because of the competition. But when one looks at a friend's yacht is it really possible to imagine them as a competitor when they love the same thing we ourselves do? One doesn't think of them as the enemy to be beaten but as a friend who is accompanying us on a day's sailing. And what a wonderful feeling seeing how the skipper-parents try to find a particular type of wood for reconstructing a piece that is broken, lost or just simply old gives. In a way they are as caring as the parent who looks for a crutch so that their convalescent son or daughter can walk.

In this type of regatta there are two quite different types of marking; that of presentation or statics (applied according to the state of preservation of the ship and the faithfulness of reconstruction if any has been done) and another that concentrates purely on the sailing, in which a compensatory formula or rating (one that aims to balance the different characteristics according to length, sail surface, etc.) is applied. Today, ships are registered according to two main groups: period ships built before 1950 or are more than 30 years old, and style or replicas, whose construction must also correspond to a traditional form of naval architecture. According to rules and regulations, other groups can be found (pleasure ship, singular, catboats, sailing boats, etc.) which often have different characteristics to boats of particular nearby ports or coasts.

The regulations, in Spain, as much in construction as in exclusively for competition are defined by the División de Barcos de Epoca (Classic Boats Division) of the RANC (Royal National Cruise Ship Association). The two most important national tests held are the 'Trofeo Almirante Conde de Barcelona', set up by S.A.R. D. Juan de Borbón y Battemberg, Conde de Barcelona, in memory of those who loved the sea and boats and brought about existence of regattas of this type. The most recent of these, the 9th, usually held in Palma, Majorca, brought together about 80 boats with rules of entry and wholly different criteria, the "Trobada de Barques de Vela Llatina" (Reunion of boats with lateen sails) as its title suggests is exclusively for boats with lateen sails, of which six have been held to date (the last with 36 boats) set in the town of Cadaqués near Girona.

On a more international level (although in the two competitions mentioned above there are always numerous foreign participants) the most important considered event is the one held every year in the waters of Sardinia, normally organised by the Club Naútico de la Costa Esmeralda in which it is said that more than a hundred boats come together.

And so it is that approaching the end we return to the beginning. Man is such an ignorant being that we value what we lose only when time has run out to get it back. When man had within his reach sailing ships of all different types, sizes and ages, he dismissed them as old, antiquated or non-profitable.

Now great effort and considerable amounts of money must be ploughed into trying to get back – something which cannot always be done – a mere crumb of that once big cake. But it has been made abundantly clear that we are the only animal that falls twice over the same stone. So just how many more times are necessary before we realise and stop making the same mistakes?

The speed that a sail boat reaches at certain moments is remarkable. Ketch *Karenita* sailing at full sail with the genoa flat out.

Bibliography

ALÁEZ ZAZUREA, José A. and MORÉN CURBE-RA, José María: *La arquitectura Naval y La Navegación en la Epoca del Descubrimiento*. E. N. "Bazán" C.M.S.A., 1992

BOUDRIOT, Jean: *The Seventy-four gun ship*. Jean Boudriot, 1986.

CARRERO BLANCO, Luis: *Arte Naval Militar*. Ed. Naval, 1965.

CIPOLLA, Carlo: *Cañones y Velas*. Ariel, 1967.

CHAPELLE, Howard I.: *The Baltimore Clipper*. Bonanza Books, 1930.

CHAPELLE, Howard I.: *The History of the American Sailing Ships*. Bonanza Books, 1935.

DUDZUS, Alfred and HENRIOT, Ernest: *Dictionary of Ship Types*. Conway Maritime Press, 1986.

HARLAND, John: *Seamanship in the Age of Sail*. Conway Maritime press, 1984.

HOWARD, Frank: *Sailing Ships of War*. Conway Maritime press, 1979.

JOBÉ, Joseph: *Los Grandes Veleros*. Published by Blume, 1973.

LLOVET, Joaquim: *Constructors Navals de l'exprovincia Maritima de Mataró 1816-1875*. Caixa d'Estalvis Laietana, 1971.

MARTHEILLE, Jean: *Memorias de un Galeote de Francia*. A.M.N.E. journal, 1961.

MARTÍNEZ-HIDALGO Y TERÁN, José María: *Enciclopedia general del Mar*. Published by Garriga, 1958.

McGREGOR, David R.: *Merchant Sailing Ships*. Conway Maritime Press, 1985.

MORDAL, Jacques: *25 Siècles de Guerre sur Mer*. Marabout Université, 1959.

ROIG, Emerencià: *La Marina Catalana del Vuitcens*. Published by Barcino, 1929.

ROIG, Emerencià: *La Pesca a Catalunya*. Published by Barcino, 1927.

VILÀ I GALÍ, Agustí M.: *La Marina Mercant de Lloret de Mar*. Ajuntament de Lloret de Mar, 1992.

WILSON, H. W.: *Les Flottes de Guerre au Combat*. Payot, 1928.

WINTER, Heinrich: *La Nau Catalana de 1450*. Diputació de Barcelona, 1986.

Various authors

A Flote; Boletín del Club de Historia y Modelismo Naval. Club de Historia y Modelismo Naval, 1991/92/93.

Les artes de la vela. Published by Raíces, 1983.

Enciclopedia Ilustrada de la Navegación a Vela. Published by Planeta, 1982.

Histoire de la Marine. Les Editions de L'Illustration, 1959.

HMS. Warrior. Pitkin Pictorials, 1991.

Marine de Plaisance. Denoël, 1978.

The Mary Rose. The Mary Rose Trust, 1992.

Portsmouth Historic Dockyard. Portsmouth Naval Base Property Trust, 1992.

Revista de Historia Naval. Instituto de Historia y Cultura Naval. Armada Española. Varios números.

Victorian Times. Tressell Publ., 1991.

Documentation, pamphlets and various magazines.